Court Hustler

Court Hustler

by Bobby Riggs

with George McGann

J. B. LIPPINCOTT COMPANY
Philadelphia and New York

PHOTO CREDITS

Photos 1, 5, 8, 9:
United Press International Photographs

Photo 3:
Stan Wayman, Time/Life Picture Agency; © 1956–72 Time, Inc.

Photos 6, 7, 10 (five photos):
Sports Illustrated Photos by Sheedy & Long; © Time, Inc.

U.S. Library of Congress Cataloging in Publication Data

Riggs, Robert Larimore, birth date
        Court hustler.

        1. Riggs, Robert Larimore, birth date
2. Tennis.   I. McGann, George.
II. Title.
GV994.R54A29   796.34'2'0924 [B]   73–13818
ISBN–0–397–00893–7

*I dedicate this book
to all the beautiful people in my family.
To my former wives, Kay and Priscilla.
To my children,
Bobby, Jr., Larry, John, Jimmy, Dolly and Billy.
To my sister, Mary Lee,
and my brothers, Sanders, David, John and Luke.*

"If I can't play for big money, I play for a little money. And if I can't play for a little money, I stay in bed that day."

—*Bobby Riggs to Mike Wallace in a TV interview.*

Court Hustler

1

AT PRECISELY 2:27 P.M. on Mother's Day, May 13, 1973, I leaped over the net, with a slight assist from my left hand, on a tennis court at San Diego Estates, California —and jumped into a whole new career.

I was fifty-five years old, a tennis has-been with one foot in the grave, who had grabbed a new lease on life.

I had just beaten Margaret Court, Australia's number-one woman player, twenty-five years my junior and the best-known mother in sports, making good on my contention that any top male tennis player, even at my advanced age, could beat any top female player.

I had put my money where my mouth is—$5,000 in cold cash—which came back to me doubled in the $10,000 winner-take-all contest, thanks to television money and other sponsorship.

I had become the hero of all middle-aged men smarting under the taunts of the Women's Libbers, the leader of Bobby's Battalions, and the undisputed number-one male chauvinist in the world.

My victory had been witnessed by 60 million TV viewers throughout the United States, Canada, Mexico and Australia, making me the best-known male tennis player of any age in the whole wide world.

As a result I was besieged by every kind of commercial offer from giving tennis lessons at $100 an hour to endorsing vitamin pills, starring in movies of my life, and challenging other women stars, all of which promised to turn me into the richest overage athlete in any sport, anywhere, anytime.

How the hell did it all happen, anyway?

I guess you could say it all began with my belief that since women don't play tennis as well as men do, they don't deserve to be paid as much as men.

As a senior player entering twenty or more tournaments a year, I resented the fact that we were playing for little or no prize money. And what's more, we had to pay our own travel expenses and hotel bills.

On the other hand, the women were cleaning up. Billie Jean King was making over $100,000 a year, which made her the highest-paid woman in any sport.

This situation griped me. What also griped me was that the ladies always played on the center court at Wimbledon and Forest Hills while we seniors were shunted off to the farthest outside courts. We were playing in virtual privacy with only our relatives looking on. I have a lot of ham in me. I didn't like being kept out of the spotlight.

I knew we were playing far better tennis on the senior circuit than you could see anywhere in women's tennis. Still, we were playing for peanuts. They were raking in the loot—and getting all the glory.

That's when I got the idea of challenging a top woman player. I was ranked number one in the fifty-and-over bracket and was even beating men five years younger. I had just as much competitive spirit as ever—especially when I got the right kind of action on the side. A good bet on myself always started the adrenalin flowing.

I was sure I could beat any woman player in the world. And if I did, my victory would put senior players—in particular, *this* senior player—in the limelight and prove that we deserved a share of the loot from advertising and television.

I decided to put $5,000 on the line, winner take all, for the match.

I also decided that Billie Jean King was my obvious opponent. She was a scrappy fighter who would put on a good show. A talkative gal, always stirring up headlines, she would generate a lot of publicity, too.

I caught up with Billie Jean at Wimbledon, in the players' dining room, at a time when she was recovering from knee surgery and temporarily out of action.

"Why don't we play a fun match—for five thousand dollars to add to the fun—on any surface you like, when you get back into action?" I asked her. She grinned.

"I'd love it," she said. "Let's do it—when I get back in shape."

I had the distinct feeling Billie Jean thought she could beat me. That was okay. I felt the same way about her.

Shortly afterward *Sports Illustrated* magazine ran an article about the growing activity in senior tennis in which my challenge to Billie Jean was quoted:

"I'd love to play her every day of the week and twice on Sunday, indoors, outdoors, on cement, clay, grass, whatever. I think I can beat her on any and all surfaces."

When the article appeared, Bob McCulloch of the Lake Havasu real-estate project, the man who bought the London Bridge and brought it to this country, called Jack Kramer, an old friend of his, and expressed interest in staging a King–Riggs match at his project. Kramer got in touch with me and said McCulloch thought the match would be a fantastic attraction and would put up $5,000 in prize money, on a winner-take-all basis.

I told Kramer I'd love to accept McCulloch's offer. But that's the last I heard of it. I presume they got in touch with Billie Jean King, but I don't know.

The next thing that happened was a long-distance phone call from Dennis Van der Meer, the California tennis pro, who asked me if I'd like to play Billie Jean for $50,000, winner take all.

"My God, I certainly would," I told him. "I agreed to play for five thousand and nothing came of it. Now you're talking about fifty thousand. How does this work?"

Van der Meer said he had a sponsor, a casino owner in Lake Tahoe, who wanted to stage the match at his site.

"Don't let this slip through your fingers," I urged Van der Meer, and offered to help the promotion in any way I could. Fifty thousand dollars! Those figures were unheard of.

Van der Meer said the casino owner was looking for TV exposure on beautiful Lake Tahoe and his site. But Van der Meer couldn't sell it to the networks. They were not interested in a match between Billie Jean and myself. When he couldn't get the TV exposure the sponsor wanted, nothing came of it. I was very disappointed.

Then I met Tony Trabert early in 1973 at the Los Angeles Tennis Club. Trabert is an old friend of mine, a former Davis Cup star and well-regarded in tennis circles. He had just been named tennis director at a new land development project called San Diego Country Estates.

He asked me what had become of the proposed match between Billie Jean and myself, and I told him the story.

"I'd like to see you revive that," Tony said. "It's a great idea. Why don't you make her an offer she can't refuse?"

We talked it over. He knew I was very unsympathetic toward women getting equal prize money with men. I said, "There's no way they deserve it. Their tennis is as different as night and day."

We didn't even think about television. We just wanted to stage the match at San Diego Country Estates for a few hundred spectators, for the publicity it would bring to the development through the press.

Larry Lurie, the public-relations man for the Estates who had brought Trabert into the development, saw far-reaching possibilities in the match and was active behind the scenes from the very beginning.

Lurie called a press conference in San Diego, attended by the wire services, the newspapers and TV, and said he had an exciting announcement to make: "Bobby Riggs, that old campaigner, ex-champion, has-been, claims that women's tennis stinks. To prove his point he has put up five thousand dollars; here's his certified check. Billie Jean King gets first crack at it but will have to answer within forty-eight hours. Otherwise Bobby will send wires to Margaret Court and four or five other women, and he will play the first one to accept the offer."

Billie Jean said she had changed her mind about the match and turned me down. With the kind of money she was making, I guess my five grand didn't look big enough to her.

The next name on the list was Margaret Smith Court, the tall thirty-year-old Australian who has won every major title in the world at least once and was currently in a hot winning streak on the Virginia Slims circuit in which she took eighty-nine out of ninety-two matches.

Margaret told us she was willing to play but wanted the match to be staged at the Jockey Club in Miami, which had offered to put up $5,000 in prize money in addition to my $5,000. As a result, the San Diego Estates people agreed to match this offer and put up $5,000 in addition to my dough. Margaret said okay.

Margaret's acceptance created enormous publicity all over the world. Newspapers headlined the forthcoming match as the Battle of the Sexes. This aroused the television people. They offered Margaret $10,000 to play on television, in addition to the $10,000 winner-take-all stake, and offered me $7,500. This meant that even if I lost the match I would still be $2,500 to the good. We both accepted the deal.

CBS scheduled the match for the afternoon of Sunday, May 13, on its full network. This happened to be Mother's Day. I immediately realized the publicity possibilities in this angle, since Margaret, the most famous mother in tennis, took her fourteen-month-old son Danny with her wherever she went.

Once the match was made, I determined to do everything possible to ensure its success. That meant playing a big role in promoting the match as well as preparing myself for it physically and tactically. Margaret Court hits the hardest ball in women's tennis, I knew, and I was not going to take her lightly.

However, I also knew about her tendency to cave in under the pressure of big matches. I determined to do what I could to build up the pressure on Margaret in all my press conferences by emphasizing the importance of the match. I called it the Match of the Century, and this caught on.

I was completely retired from business, newly divorced and living with my older brother David at the beautiful Park Newport apartment complex in Newport Beach, California. So I was able to give the upcoming match all my time and attention.

I had eight weeks to get ready and was determined to be in the best shape possible for a man of fifty-five. On the advice of my friend Dick Moody I went to Rheo Blair, the Hollywood nutritional scientist whose techniques have rejuvenated Lawrence Welk, Liberace and other theatrical personalities. Blair's method includes lots of pills, loaded with vitamins, germ oil, liver extract and predigested protein, as well as daily massage and exercises.

Blair knows nothing about tennis. His field is body development. He has developed weight lifters by the score and just as many candidates for the Mr. America muscle contests. In fact he offered to give me a body like Mr. America in five weeks, so that I could pose as a centerfold nude in *Cosmopolitan* or *Playgirl*. Even at my age he said he could do it for me. But I turned him down on that. I just wanted to play tennis.

I first checked on Blair's methods with Dr. Omar Fareed in Los Angeles, who said there was nothing in the program that could harm me.

Blair's fee was $5,000. People said, "You're crazy. You can get vitamins in a drugstore for thirty dollars." I paid Blair $2,500 in advance and said, "If I win you get the other twenty-five hundred. If I lose, you get no more money. If you think your technique can help me that much, you should go along with this proposition."

Blair agreed to take the gamble. He gave me a valise filled with pills; his treatment required me to take 415 of them every day. That's a lot of pills. People asked me, "When do you find time to play tennis?"

Along with the pills I got Blair's personal consultation, his expertise on nutrition, his advice on training, exercise and physical fitness. He supervised the trainer who gave me two hours of massage every day. Blair is a great believer in moving the blood around—"pushing the blood," as he calls it—getting it circulating, moving and flowing into the system. He gave me special exercises to make me more limber. Tennis players have a tendency to stiffen up in the back, as Jack Kramer and Rod Laver have reason to know.

I had to jog around the school track near my home in Newport Beach, covering at least a mile every day. I also went on a diet of straight proteins and dairy products.

I weighed 160 pounds when I started the Blair treatment. A few hours after the match against Margaret Court, eight weeks later, I weighed 144 pounds. That was my weight in my days on the pro tour, but I hadn't been anywhere near that low in twenty-five years.

I also imposed a monastic program on myself, giving up my bachelor life of drinking and dating. "No Booze, No Broads, Vows Riggs" was the way one newspaper described it. At any rate sex was out for the duration. I believe I benefited, at least psychologically.

I wanted to be able to say afterward, if Margaret beat me, that it was because she was a better player than I was at this time in my career. I didn't want to look back and say to myself, "If you had only trained harder, jogged daily, not had those drinks and those dates, you wouldn't have lost it."

Furthermore, I have always believed that you get out of something what you put into it. If you want to be a winner, you have to be dedicated and willing to sacrifice smaller pleasures for the big return.

I realized I had a lot riding on this match. It could reinstate me in the eyes of the sports public as a major figure and mean a lot of money for me. I didn't need the immediate financial reward that winning the match would bring me, but it could lead to commercial endorsements, as well as more matches against women. It could put me back in the limelight again, after twenty years in business, away from sports.

So I wanted very much to win it. I didn't like the idea of losing, after what I had been saying about the quality of women's tennis. If I lost, I would be known as a fifty-five-year-old bum who had opened his mouth and put his foot in it. I would become the laughingstock of tennis.

I also felt that I was carrying a banner for all middle-aged men. The Women's Libbers had labeled me a male chauvinist, to which I replied, "Okay, as long as I'm the number-one male chauvinist." This was all tongue-in-cheek as far as I was concerned. But I felt it really would be a blow to men's morale everywhere if I got knocked off by Margaret.

The timing of the match could not have been better, in capturing the attention of the public. It came at the height of the Women's Lib movement and seemed to strike a chord with all women, Libbers or not. So it attracted the attention of people who ordinarily never look at the sports pages or watch sports on TV.

It also came at a time when interest in the game of tennis was at an all-time high, when tennis was the "in" game and the smart thing to do was to carry a tennis racket with you wherever you went, even if you couldn't use the darn thing. Girls were dressing in tennis clothes who never struck a ball in their lives. The Great Gatsby look, based on tennis styles of the twenties, was sweeping the country.

To keep the publicity pot boiling, I went around

scouting Margaret on the Virginia Slims tour, watching her in action and giving my reactions to sports writers on the scene. I was amazed to find myself the center of attraction wherever I went. The match really was building up as the Match of the Century. The big news agencies, the Associated Press, United Press International and Reuters cooperated nicely in my PR activities. They quoted at length my comments on the match, which duly appeared in thousands of newspapers in this country and abroad and were repeated by radio and TV sportscasters. Nothing like this had ever happened to me when I was Wimbledon champion in 1939 or when I was the world professional champion after World War II.

The first place I watched Margaret was in Richmond, Virginia. I had seen her play often and there was no need really to analyze her game, but I made a great show of being impressed by what I saw.

I protested to reporters that Jimmy the Greek, the Las Vegas betting authority, was all wrong in making me a 7-to-5 favorite to beat Margaret.

"I think it's an even-money bet," I insisted. "She plays like a man, I play like a woman. She's younger, stronger and faster than I am. She's got a better serve, a better volley and a better overhead. She's got me beaten in every department except maybe in thinking, strategy and experience."

But I also told the reporters that I had detected a weakness in her game—she could not handle soft shots, since she thrived on her opponent's speed.

I also made no secret of the fact that I intended to soft-ball her to death come Mother's Day. I made no secret at any time of my game plan, how I intended to use lobs, drop shots and floaters to break up her attacking tactics, and ball control to reduce my errors.

The reporters were always looking for an angle in everything I did and said. I was telling them the truth, but they tried to find some deep, devious plot behind my words. It was all right with me. It built up the publicity and my image as a hustler, which I've long since learned to live with.

Take the business of the surface we were to play on at San Diego Estates. It was fast cement, infinitely more suited to Margaret's game, with her powerful serve and volley, than to my retrieving tactics. On cement she would have every opportunity to put the ball away, whereas I would have had a better chance to defend on a slower surface such as clay.

I went along with the cement court. But when I asked that it be resurfaced for our match, the press leaped on me and everyone accused me of seeking an unfair advantage by slowing it down.

The truth was that I wanted the court to look better. It had been down for quite a while and had been played a lot. It was dusty, and the sun had washed out its original bright green color. I wanted a fresh green court to play on so that the balls would stand out against it. I also asked that it be treated to make it play slower, since I thought Margaret had too much of an advantage the way it was, but when this was turned down I accepted the decision.

However, when the San Diego people did a resurfacing job a few days before the match to improve its appearance, this also had the effect of somewhat slowing it down. The press immediately accused me of unfair tactics. The court was fine. So far as I know, Margaret never made a complaint about the surface, before or after the match.

There was a lot written about the choice of balls, too, with the inference that I had pulled off a big hustle to get the ones I wanted. Here is what really happened.

I had been practicing with the standard Spalding ball that I use in our friendly betting games in California and am accustomed to. About a week before the match Tony Trabert, who has a long-time connection with the Wilson Sporting Goods Company, told me that the heavy-duty Wilson ball had been chosen for the match.

I tried the selected ball but found it heavy and soggy. I went to Tony and said, "I'm psyched out on that ball. It could make all the difference in this match."

Tony listened to my complaint and came up with a reasonable answer. "Well, in that case we'll switch to the championship Wilson ball, which is quite a bit faster."

I agreed to this and Tony went off to telephone Margaret, who was up in Berkeley practicing with Dennis Van der Meer.

Tony came back with the news that when Margaret and Van der Meer heard that I wanted to use the light ball, they protested that they had been practicing with the heavy-duty ball and insisted on using it.

"So I've decided you'll have to flip a coin," Tony said, "and whoever wins the flip will have the right to select the ball."

I accused Tony of reneging on his word that we would use the faster Wilson ball. We had quite an argument about this but I lost out. I agreed to the toss.

Meanwhile I had continued using the heavy-duty ball in practice, changing the gut in my racket to an imported brand better suited to that ball. I found that I was now able to handle the heavy-duty ball just as well as I had the lighter ball.

So when the time came to flip for the ball, I said to Tony, "There's no question but that if Margaret wins the flip, we'll use the heavy-duty ball, is there?"

"That's right," he replied.

"Well, if I win the flip, I'll tell you which ball I'm going to use, but I'm not declaring myself in advance."

As it turned out, Margaret won the flip and chose the heavy-duty ball, as expected.

Right away, suspicion arose that I had wanted the heavy-duty balls all along and had somehow maneuvered Margaret into choosing them. The truth was that I had originally opposed them, but when it came down to the flip, if I had won I might well have chosen them. However, it was because I had gotten used to them by then, not because I preferred them all along.

As usual, the hustle angle, not the truth, made news.

Opinions over the result of the upcoming match were sharply divided, usually along strictly male-female lines. In my interviews I called it a mystery match, since nothing like it had ever happened before in any sport—man versus woman, age versus youth.

My nineteen-year-old daughter, Dolly, who came out to California from school in the east to see the match, was torn by it. She encouraged me, but she did say, "If you weren't my father, I'd be rooting for Margaret Court."

The New York Times conducted a survey of well-known tennis authorities. Fred Perry, my old opponent on the pro tour, predicted, "She won't win a game." Harry Hopman, former Australian Davis Cup captain, was just as positive. "The only way Riggs could lose is to break a leg."

Don Budge, Billy Talbert and Gardnar Mulloy, three of my oldest friends and competitors, also predicted I would win easily.

This kind of talk infuriated a lot of women, notably Margaret's fellow professionals on the Virginia Slims tour, who had been taking a steady beating from her.

"Why should we have to justify ourselves against an old, obnoxious has-been like Riggs?" asked Rosemary Casals. "He can't hear, can't see, walks like a duck and is an idiot besides."

I met Julie Heldman, another touring pro, and asked her what she thought of my chances. Not very good, she replied.

Did she think I had an outside chance?

"Yes—way outside," Julie answered.

Pancho Gonzales was among the men who thought Margaret would beat me. Pancho Segura was afraid to bet on me after Rosemary Casals warned him, "Margaret will kill Bobby."

Dennis Van der Meer of course picked Margaret.

As her part-time coach, Van der Meer told people, "We've got him figured out.

"I saw Bobby's weakness," he added. "It's his forehand. He can do a lot of things with his backhand but he can just hit his forehand one way."

The fact is that my forehand has always been my principal strength.

For some reason a lot of well-known black people picked Margaret—Althea Gibson, Bill Cosby and O. J. Simpson among them.

Hank Greenberg, the Hall of Fame baseball slugger, an old betting crony of mine from New York, also defected and backed Margaret—but not with me, I'm sorry to say. I'd have won a bundle from him.

The good women players felt so strongly they refused to practice with me. Karen Susman, former Wimbledon champion, told me, "I won't do anything that might help you or hurt Margaret."

My old pal from Cleveland, Jack March, donned a wig and women's tennis dress to play me, but it wasn't quite the same as playing a woman.

I understand that a lot of the girls on the pro tour pooled their money to get a big bet down on Margaret. Women's Libbers bet their men friends that Margaret would put me in my place. It's too bad the off-track betting shops in New York confine betting to the horses. They could have done a lot of business handling the action on our match.

The betting wasn't confined to this country either. In Australia, Margaret's homeland, where betting is legal, the bookmakers in Tattersall's Club made me the favorite at odds of 7 to 4. Those bookies didn't let sentiment or patriotism alter their judgment. They went along with their male chauvinist instincts. A major

Australian television network, Channel Nine, carried the match live from California. It was 6:30 A.M. Monday morning in Australia when the match started, but millions of Aussies got out of bed to watch it. The match was repeated twice more that day for the benefit of late sleepers.

In my comments I tried to give the impression that the pressure was all on Margaret. I insisted she had everything to lose, as the women's champion upholding the reputation of her sex, while I had nothing to lose.

But as the match drew near, my own tension rose. The phone calls and interviews never stopped. I was getting worried. One reporter tried to get me to admit that I was feeling the pressure. Old guys lose their nerve, he needled me.

"Look at Ben Hogan and Sam Snead. They can't putt anymore. You haven't played an important match in twenty-three years, so the pressure's going to be on you. The stuff you've been playing is Mickey Mouse tennis."

I argued him down, but I was beginning to wonder if I could keep up the pace and still reach the right kind of peak for the match. The phone rang day and night at the apartment in Newport Beach, where my brother Dave was acting as a buffer for me. I tried to go into hiding but it was impossible to get away from it all.

I moved down to San Diego Estates and the thing got worse. The switchboard lighted up day and night. They were calling from all over the place—Denver, Miami, London, Sydney—and all of them wanted a taped interview. I was groggy from answering the same

27

questions: Are you a male chauvinist? Will you beat her? What are the odds? Does women's tennis really stink?

Things were not going well in my practice sessions with Hans Wichary, a local pro. When I ran after the ball, my legs felt like they were about to cave in. It was like running in quicksand. I was missing the old skippiness.

Then two things happened that eased the tension and restored my confidence.

I learned that Margaret had left the Virginia Slims tour a week early and gone to Berkeley to prepare for our match and to develop a game plan with the help of Dennis Van der Meer.

"That's the best news I've heard in a long time," I told my pals. "When the world champion has to consult a teaching pro about how to play me, I know she's in trouble. Now I'm beginning to breathe easier."

The other thing that changed my frame of mind was the arrival of my friend Lornie Kuhle, the young pro at the Las Vegas Country Club, who had taken a few days off to help me sharpen my game for Margaret.

"I want to work on my airtight game," I told Lornie, who knew exactly what I was talking about. "I want to put all my defensive theories into effect against Margaret."

For the two days leading up to the match we practiced specific formations and tactics. Lornie, who hits a much harder ball than Margaret, pounded serves at me from both boxes. He rushed the net, so that I could practice my lobs and high floaters. I tried short angle shots and various kinds of spin. I varied the length and depth of my shots. I concentrated on hitting to his backhand.

"I want you to hit the ball as hard as you can," I told him, "so that it will seem that she's hitting soft shots by comparison."

I worked on my quickness, footwork and court coverage.

On the last day of hard practice I began to feel the cumulative effect of all the preparation. I felt ready.

My practice sessions drew a throng of curious spectators each day, mainly the advance guard of reporters and television people who were flying in from all over the world. Our match was to be played the same afternoon as the finals of world championship tennis in Dallas, in which Arthur Ashe and Stan Smith battled for a $50,000 first prize. But a lot of the top sports writers in the country elected to skip Dallas and cover our Match of the Century instead.

The writers were not overly impressed with my practice sessions. They saw Lornie pounding serves at me, overpowering me from the net and chasing me back and forth along the baseline. They did not know that we were practicing patterns of play, and I did not tell them. I looked like a middle-aged guy who was in over his head against a tough young pro half his age. Some of the reporters who had picked me to beat Margaret were beginning to have second thoughts.

These doubts increased when Margaret arrived in San Diego Estates from her week of practice with Van der Meer and went out on the court with Tony Trabert two days before the match.

Margaret was hitting the ball beautifully. Her

service was sharp, her volleys even sharper and her powerful ground strokes were finding the corners. She seemed to handle Tony's best shots with ease.

She also practiced with Vicki Berner, another hard-hitting member of the Virginia Slims troupe, and their sessions produced a lot of lively exchanges.

Margaret impressed a lot of the onlookers as well as the press with her power stroking. But to my mind she was practicing all wrong for the match. Hitting against Tony Trabert and Vicki Berner the last two days was not the smart thing to do. They are both big hitters who cannot alter their pace or style. They certainly weren't giving Margaret the kind of soft stuff she was going to get from me—and that I had threatened all along to use against her. And evidently Van der Meer, whom she depended upon so much in the final week, didn't attempt to play my game against her—or couldn't play it.

At any rate, Margaret looked very impressive in practice. She was getting great speed and pace on each ball from Tony and Vicki and could play her own naturally powerful game. The onlookers, notably the tennis reporters, were completely taken in. In a poll of the press, including radio and TV representatives, made the night before the match, Margaret was favored overwhelmingly, by a margin of 3 to 1. These guys, and they were among the best in the business, simply couldn't believe I could cope with Margaret's obviously greater aggressiveness and power.

The setting of the match was as unusual as the match itself. San Diego Estates, a luxury housing development in the early stages of building, lies in the

Cuyamaca Mountains about fifty miles northeast of San Diego. It is surrounded by several Indian reservations, and the road through nearby Wildcat Canyon is supposed to be used as a midnight drop for narcotics smugglers from Mexico. The reporters, radio and TV newscasters had a lot of fun describing the background, which looked like a location for a Hollywood movie. One Australian correspondent noted that John Wayne, who arrived to hand out the prize money at the end of the match, was a comforting sight—the Duke's presence would keep our Indian neighbors from staging an uprising.

Another writer recalled that the legendary grudge match of the twenties between Suzanne Lenglen and Helen Wills, the only meeting between the two arch rivals, had also been played in what was then an out-of-the-way spot, the little town of Cannes on the French Riviera.

The players, press and officials connected with the match were comfortably housed in the main clubhouse of the San Vicente Golf Course, part of the land project. I was staying there in a suite, with my brother Dave and Lornie Kuhle. Margaret, her husband Barry and their young son, Danny, were housed a few doors away. We took our meals separately in the same big dining room. The atmosphere was friendly and free and easy between Margaret's camp and mine.

One night I came home a bit late and walked into a room through an open door. I was well into the suite before I realized it wasn't mine. Margaret Court was sitting there, playing with Danny.

"Oh, Margaret, I'm so sorry—I've got the wrong

31

room," I said as I backed out. My own suite was a few doors along the path.

When word of this got out, I was again accused of gamesmanship, of trying deliberately to upset my opponent by stumbling into her room.

One night Danny was sitting in a high chair in the dining room, banging a glass with a spoon.

"Hush, Danny," his mother said. "You make more noise than Bobby Riggs."

Danny wore a big button that the Court followers were handing out: "Bobby Riggs—Bleah!"

Somebody told me a firm in Toronto put out fifty thousand of these buttons and sold them all over Canada and the United States. I didn't realize there were that many Women's Libbers around.

Another night at dinner, I picked up a plate of pills that I had not yet downed and carried them over to Margaret's table. I offered her the plate but she just laughed and refused them.

As far as I was concerned, our relations couldn't have been more cordial. Margaret's husband, a big yachtsman from Western Australia, was equally friendly. We even had a beer together after the match.

However, Margaret's lawyer, Larry Krieger, proved anything but friendly in the final discussions we had about the conduct of the match.

Krieger, who is also a USLTA official in New York, flew out to San Diego several days beforehand. Along with Barry Court, he attended a meeting of the two sides called by Tony Trabert a few hours before the match. Margaret was not there. I attended with Lornie Kuhle.

Tony suggested that in order to solve any problems that might arise during the match, a referee be named as the final authority. Tony nominated Jack Kramer for the job, and I seconded the motion. I regard Jack as one of the outstanding individuals in tennis, who has the good of the game at heart.

To my surprise Krieger jumped to his feet and said "I protest strongly." Krieger thought Kramer was prejudiced against women because he had been involved in the prize-money dispute in Los Angeles which led to the formation of the Virginia Slims tour.

Krieger said that the umpire selected for the match, a San Diego pro and tennis official named Ben Press, would be capable of handling any disputes that might arise. I went along with this.

Krieger also made a pointed remark about gamesmanship and expressed the hope that the match would be conducted in a serious manner. I seconded that sentiment too.

I think Krieger would now agree that the match was played with all the decorum he wanted.

Jack Kramer, by the way, bought fifty tickets for the match, the gate receipts of which went to a charitable cause and not to Margaret or myself.

Besides Jack, a good many tennis personalities found their way over the narrow mountain road to the site of the match, as well as thousands of tennis fans, who began arriving as early as 9 A.M., four hours before it started.

My nutritionist, Rheo Blair, got there the night before, to make sure that I was in bed early for a good night's sleep and to fix up a baked potato and avocado salad meal for me on a portable burner. He was doing everything he could to see that his $2,500 gamble paid off.

I had told Lornie Kuhle that I wanted to have three practice sessions on Sunday morning. I am a slow starter and I wanted to start the match fully warmed up.

Lornie woke me up bright and early. He was unusually excited.

"Bobby!" he shouted. "I dreamed about the match —and you won it six–two, six–one!"

"With a score like that it's got to be a dream," I replied. But I got excited too. I'm a great believer in dreams.

After our first practice session that morning, I got on the phone to Jack Dreyfus in New York. Dreyfus, who founded the Wall Street firm bearing his name, is an avid tennis buff and a high bettor. I have been playing and betting with Jack for years. On the phone I told Jack I had heard on the grapevine that he expected Margaret to beat me.

"No, Bobby," he replied. "I know you can take her."

I was disappointed. I reminded Jack that I had won a bet from him on a senior tennis match the year before against Torsten Johansson, after calling him long-distance from California.

"You know how superstitious I am," I told him. "How about repeating the bet with me, for good luck?"

Jack laughed good-naturedly. "If you feel that way, of course I'll bet you," he said. "But I won't go higher than a thousand. And I'll be rooting for you anyway."

The bet gave me a confident feeling. It seemed a

good omen. It was not much money, but I did not need a big bet to get in the mood to beat Margaret. I had too many other things going for me on this match. I had all the incentive I needed, without my usual big action on the side.

As extra insurance I got in touch with Louis Sacco, a senior tennis player in San Diego, who had never won a bet from me in his life. He agreed to back Margaret.

"Thanks, Louie," I said. "That really puts the kiss of death on her."

The day of the match was perfect for tennis. Although it was foggy in the morning, the sun came out brilliantly just before we started hitting up. Oddly enough it disappeared again shortly after the match. There was a mild breeze blowing, which cooled the spectators but didn't affect the flight of the ball.

The day had started badly for Margaret. Young Danny got up early, picked up his mother's favorite sneakers and threw them in the toilet. I guess they dried out by game time.

Although Margaret later complained about a carnival atmosphere surrounding the match, I thought it was well staged and went off as smoothly as a Wimbledon final. A full complement of linesmen and lineswomen—equally divided—was on hand, and a professional umpire was in the chair. There wasn't a doubtful call.

I had let it be known beforehand that I wanted a second with me on the side of the court, to help me analyze Margaret's game and if necessary help me change my strategy if I got into trouble. He could also help me physically, with quick massages of the neck, back, arms and legs during changeovers and between sets. I chose Hans Wichary for this job, and he was backed up by Lornie Kuhle, who sat just behind us and joined in our courtside conferences.

Margaret asked Van der Meer to act as her second, and he sat at courtside throughout the match, on the other side of the umpire's stand from Wichary.

We got a big break on TV the afternoon of Mother's Day. The final match of the world championship tennis series in Dallas started an hour and a half before our match and provided a perfect lead-in, ending just fifteen minutes before we came out on the court at San Diego Estates. Those who watched Stan Smith and Arthur Ashe in Dallas on the NBC network had time for a beer before switching to us on CBS. I am afraid my friend Lamar Hunt was not too happy about the comparative audience ratings for the two networks. NBC had a 4.5-point share of the viewing audience in the United States, according to the *Hollywood Reporter*, while our match attracted a whopping 39-point share. An estimated 60 million people watched us play on live camera in North America and Australia. Interest in the outcome was at a fantastically high pitch. The finals of the Southern California tennis championships were postponed two hours so that the players could watch our match.

Margaret came out on the court first, wearing a yellow and green dress designed by Teddy Tinling with her name stitched on the collar in big letters. Tinling flew in from Tokyo just to see that it fit right. The colors were copied from the Australian wattle, the national flower.

36

I walked onto the court in a powder-blue warm-up suit, carrying a bouquet of twelve red roses in my arms. I had attached a card to the bouquet, reading "For one of the all-time greats in tennis who is just as great a mother. Good luck." I handed her the bouquet at the side of the court.

Margaret responded in ladylike fashion, giving me the kind of curtsy she uses when facing the royal box at Wimbledon.

Pat Sumerall, the former football star, was doing the TV announcing at courtside.

"Do you think the roses will soften her up?" I asked Pat.

"I don't think so," he replied curtly.

Naturally the bouquet of roses was picked up by the press as another hustle. But it was a sincere gesture on my part to a lovely mother, and it added to the fun aspect of the match. According to letters I received, the television audience got a big charge out of it, and that was my idea. I doubt that it had any psychological effect on Margaret.

Because of the television timetable, we were allowed only a brief warm-up. It suited me, since I had been practicing with Lornie Kuhle all morning. But I think Margaret was a bit surprised when the umpire called, "Players ready," after we had knocked only a few balls back and forth from the baseline.

I had been counting on the pressure to get to Margaret in this match, and we had barely started when I realized she was as tight as a drum.

She was playing fast—too fast. And my game went from soft to softer. I gave her floaters, spin shots, drop shots. I concentrated on her backhand and stayed away from her forehand, her best shot.

She continually missed her first serve, and her second ball was easy for me to handle. My serve fooled her. She didn't realize that my spin serve was going to be so difficult to handle. It was not hard to get into play. But it was difficult for her to attack it. I was serving wide to her on both sides, so she couldn't come to the net behind her returns. She was so surprised by my serve that she was even dumping the second ball into the net.

Margaret got only one point in the first game against my serve. In the second game she came up to the net behind serve and I tossed her a midcourt lob which she smashed into the bottom of the net. That shook her up. She double-faulted the next point and I broke through for a 2-to-0 lead. She managed to hold her next service game by coming to net but had no confidence up there. She played the rest of the match mainly from the baseline, making the cardinal mistake of playing *my* game, not her own.

When I got to 5 to 1, I was so loose and confident that I stopped concentrating. I had several girl friends here and there in the stands, and I started looking around for them. I spotted a tennis pal from Newport Beach and smiled and waved at him.

I tried a crazy shot from the baseline that I mis-hit to my feet. What I was trying to do was to spin the ball to land on Margaret's side of the net and bounce back on mine. It's a trick shot that often works for me, but not this time. Too bad. I wanted to impress that big TV audience.

I really didn't care if Margaret broke my serve. She got that game on my errors. But at 5 to 2 I concentrated on her backhand, and she put my floaters into the net. I had the first set 6 to 2.

But I was still cautious. I thought that Margaret must surely have lost the butterflies in her stomach by now and would make her move, change her tactics, do something to try to turn the match around. I don't know what Van der Meer told her between sets, but if it was to change her strategy, she didn't listen.

After winning her service at love in the second game of the final set, Margaret again retreated to the baseline, where she lost most exchanges with me. I changed pace on my service, knocking two aces past her, back to back, which caught her flat-footed.

At 5 to 1 I looked at the scoreboard and eased up, as I had in the first set. I thought the television show might be ending too soon. I was enjoying myself so much that I wanted the match to go on. The ham in me was showing. A lot of people said to me afterward, "You tried to give her the game," but that wasn't exactly true. I wasn't making an all-out effort to take it, though. The game went to deuce five times. Margaret had four chances to break my serve but missed every one. I finished off the match with a big serve down the middle, exactly fifty-seven minutes after it began.

I ran to the net, jumped over and put my arm around Margaret. I said a few words to try to comfort her, but she was broken up by the one-sided score of 6–2, 6–1. I really sympathized with her. I have never in my life tried to humiliate an opponent, and

I certainly had tried to give Margaret a chance to improve the score.

All I had wanted to do was prove my point about women's tennis as compared to men's. I did that. I was genuinely sorry that a lovely girl like Margaret had to suffer as much as she did afterward.

However, in the various press conferences that went on for hours afterward I was puzzled by one thing Margaret said—that she had not been prepared for the match and didn't anticipate my slow stuff. She said she didn't expect me to play like a woman. In London a week later she called me sneaky.

I wondered where Margaret had been for the previous two months, when I was telling the whole world exactly how I intended to play her. I had disclosed my game plan in detail and stuck to it. I wondered, too, why Van der Meer hadn't told Margaret how I would play her.

Maybe my reputation for hustling was such that they didn't believe what I said. But if the match was a hustle, it was an honest one. The *real* court hustle was telling the truth from the beginning.

Another thing. Margaret said she couldn't see the ball, that it looked like a Ping-Pong ball coming toward her. I can't explain this, since most people say my soft stuff comes up like a watermelon.

I guess it was just nerves on Margaret's part. She must have been suffering from what one newspaper called Riggsitis.

This whole business of being called a hustler is part of what I call the Riggs Mythology. It all started about twenty years ago, when I retired from tennis and took up golf. *Life* magazine ran an article about some genuine hustlers in golf and printed my picture along with theirs. The article was careful to say that I was *not* a golf hustler, but people preferred to think otherwise.

I think of a hustler as someone who makes a living by gambling and taking advantage of people through deception. Minnesota Fats in the movies was that kind of hustler.

I am not a hustler in that sense of the term. I have been a world champion since the age of twenty-one. There is no way I can hide my identity.

Far from being an advantage, the term hustler has always penalized me. In golf I had to play below my true handicap in order to get a game. In tennis I am always giving handicaps that force me to play at my very best—or better than my best. But I don't mind. I love the challenge.

The word hustler does not offend me, although some of my close friends and members of my family resent it. I think of it more as a term of endearment now—like being called an old pro.

People call me a hustler when they really mean a bettor. I like to play all kinds of games besides tennis and golf—backgammon, gin rummy, shooting baskets, pitching cards in a hat, you name it. But I've got to have a bet going in order to play my best.

This has been true all my life. Half the fun and excitement of games for me is the negotiating that goes on in advance. The bigger the bet, the better I play. But it is often hard to get an opponent to raise the stakes to the level I like. So I have learned to appeal to the larceny in everyone's soul. I have to offer a bargain —big odds or a big handicap of some kind—to get an opponent to make a sizable bet. I can turn a ten-dollar bettor into a hundred-dollar bettor if I can persuade him he can't possibly lose with the handicap he's getting from me.

By giving big odds and big handicaps I not only get the kind of bet I want, I also get the kind of challenge I need.

One of the very first times I stepped on a golf course, I was playing with the club president. He was a middle-aged man still shooting in the eighties. I hadn't even broken a hundred. I was hacking the ball all over the place. After a couple of holes I said to him, "How about a little bet on the next hole?"

"Oh, no," he replied, "I can't bet—I have high blood pressure."

"Well," I told him, "I have to bet—I've got low blood pressure."

I love pressure. I'm used to it, after a lifetime of big-time tennis and big-money golf matches. But the ordinary individual chokes and folds under the pressure of important matches. That's how I win the big ones. That's why I can afford to give so many bargains to my opponents. I lean over backward to give them the best of it. Still they lose.

And when they do, they tell everybody, "I was hustled by Bobby Riggs."

2

I HAVE BEEN BETTING on myself, in one way or another, ever since I was a kid growing up in Los Angeles. Almost the first memory I have of anything—I suppose I was about four years old—is having a footrace with another kid in the neighborhood. My four older brothers were keen about all kinds of sports and they liked to test my ability, even at that tender age.

I was always very fast on my feet, and my brothers decided to give my opponent a handicap of a few yards' start, to be fair to him. Then they gave me an incentive to win. "If you beat him, we'll take you to the ballgame today, to see the Angels play." They added, "If you lose, you'll get a kick in the ass." With that kind of incentive, I went out and beat the other kid easily.

That was the beginning. After that it was pitching pennies to a line or playing blackjack for pennies and nickels. I grew up playing penny-ante poker, in between sets, waiting for a court in the public parks. Those were the Depression years and nobody had any money.

Balls were always a big problem and you didn't get new ones very often. They were three for a dollar. So if I didn't have a dollar in my pocket—and I never did —I would play the other kid for new balls. I had to make damn sure I won, so I picked my opponents carefully. I got to be clever at appraising the other fellow's ability, a trait that has stood me in good stead all my life.

My father, Gideon Wright Riggs, was a minister in the Church of Christ, a strict fundamentalist sect which frowns on smoking, drinking, dancing and even organ music. Gambling, of course, was as bad a sin as you could find. My dad wouldn't allow a deck of cards in the house. So my brothers and I did all our cardplaying elsewhere, usually in a shack in the backyard, which was unofficial headquarters for the kids in the neighborhood. Every once in a while, Dad would catch us with the cards and would tear them up and give us another lecture on the evils of gambling. But I'm afraid the lesson was lost on me. I've never felt there was anything wrong with gambling as long as you don't get in over your head and start betting the rent money.

I think of myself as someone who was programmed to become an athlete of some kind. It was just accidental that I took to tennis; it might just as well have been baseball or track or football or basketball, although my small size would have been a disadvantage in most other sports.

In our middle-class Los Angeles family of six boys and one girl, we all led an active outdoor life centered around sports of all kinds. I was the baby of the family.

My earliest memories are of our large rambling house in Lincoln Heights and the games we played, the lively competition and my efforts to keep up with my older brothers. The good California climate enabled us to play outdoors every day in the year, and we didn't miss many. However, Father insisted that we attend Sunday school and remain relatively quiet on the Sabbath. Anyone who knows me knows how I love to talk, and this trait I come by honestly from my father, who was also something of an athlete in his youth. It may surprise others who know me only by reputation to learn that I have always been affiliated with a church and even taught Sunday school when my kids were growing up on Long Island.

My father, who was fifty years old when I was born, lived to see me become a big success in tennis. He was a great character. Cataracts cost him the sight of one eye when I was just a kid, and gradually the sight in the other eye dimmed as well. But he always came to the big tournaments where I was playing in Southern California. He took great delight in my matches. He sat right on the sideline, completely blind, listening to the umpire calling the score.

Friends would come up to him and say, "Congratulations on Bobby's win." He would smile broadly and shake their hands.

My brothers instilled in me the drive to compete and excel. They were good teachers, excellent athletes themselves. They showed me the finer points of games. I was wiry, fast on my feet, and played an outstanding game at every age level. They even made a boxer out of me. I was the best six-year-old fighter in Lincoln

Heights. I took to all games naturally and always had a good eye for the ball, no matter what the sport. I am still willing to back myself at foul shooting, for the right shade of odds.

So by the time I took up tennis, at twelve years of age, I was quite an experienced competitor, thanks to my brothers, our sports environment and the California weather.

People have said to me that I must have been a million-to-one shot to become a world champion. But my answer is that there were no more than a dozen or so kids in the world who had my opportunities at sport at such an early age and got the kind of coaching and competition that were available in California at the time I came along. I feel I should not get all the credit for achieving what I did in tennis. I was one of a large group of outstanding tennis players who came from the same environment—Ellsworth Vines, Don Budge, Gene Mako, Jack Kramer, Ted Schroeder, Pancho Gonzales, Welby Van Horn, Joe Hunt and later Dennis Ralston and Erik Van Dillen. We all had a natural aptitude for the game, it's true, but nowhere else in the world, with the exception of Australia, were the opportunities so great to excel in tennis as in California.

My introduction to the game was casual—no one had even suggested tennis to me before. My brother John, who was not quite as accomplished an athlete as the others, decided to go out for the high-school tennis team. He began practicing at a nearby municipal playground court. I wandered over there one day and became fascinated as I watched John playing. I begged him to let me try my hand. I borrowed a racket from a boy I knew and went out on the court in my bare feet, since I had no tennis shoes.

As I was awkwardly banging the ball back and forth, Dr. Esther Bartosh, a woman who was to have a great influence on my life, stopped to watch.

"How old is your brother?" she asked John.

"Just turned twelve."

"That's the perfect age to start anyone in tennis. If you like, I'll be glad to help him."

Dr. Bartosh, an anatomy instructor at the University of Southern California, was the third-ranking woman player in Los Angeles.

I was excited over the prospect of taking lessons. Somehow I knew after that first experience on a tennis court that I had found the sport for me.

On the way home John impressed me with the lucky break I was getting and the necessity for regular practice with Dr. Bartosh's help. I didn't know how I'd explain where I was going after school to my fellow baseball players. They certainly wouldn't accept tennis as an excuse for skipping our regular games. I took plenty of ribbing when they found out about my new sport. It was considered a sissy game, not in the same category as the rougher sports we loved so much.

My immediate problem was to acquire a racket of my own. As I was pondering ways and means of solving it, I got into a game of marbles with one of my schoolmates. At the end of a half hour I had won all his marbles. Whereupon he said, "Bobby, my sister has a tennis racket she never uses. How about me trading her racket for the marbles you just won?"

"You got a deal, Jimmy. Go get the racket."

That's how I acquired my first racket, which was pretty beaten up and too small for me. But it was good enough to get me started. What's more, I won back all the marbles from Jimmy the next time we played.

Dr. Bartosh taught me the proper grips and was insistent on the right stroking, taking the racket back in preparation for the ball, and correct footwork. She was patient and I was an eager pupil. After two or three months of daily instruction she entered my name in a local country club tournament. I got to the finals, losing to a boy named Bob Underwood, who was wealthy and well coached. In my next tournament, a few weeks later, I turned the tables on Underwood, beating him in the finals.

His mother was incensed by Bob's defeat at the hands of an unknown player who had just taken up the game. She complained to the officials that her son had been unable to concentrate. This was because of the noise made by a gang of my friends who had come to see what the sissy sport was all about. They booed all Underwood's errors and cheered my winning points.

That was the start of a series of wins which lasted unbroken for two years in the thirteen-and-under division. With Dr. Bartosh's help, my game steadily improved. But the Southern California Tennis Association and its dictatorial head, Perry Jones, were anything but impressed by me or my game.

Jones was a bit of a snob who was more concerned about a youngster's family background and how he dressed than about his tennis ability. He ran the tennis association from his private office at the exclusive Los Angeles Tennis Club, and it was a one-man show. He liked his young tennis players to be tall, immaculate in white tennis clothes, and respectfully polite.

I was short—five feet, seven and one-half inches when I stopped growing—my tennis gear sometimes needed laundering, and I always spoke up to Jones, letting him know how I felt about what I considered discrimination against kids like myself, who didn't happen to come from Pasadena or Beverly Hills or the other upper-class areas of Los Angeles.

"Riggs is too short" was the opinion of Jones and the other Establishment figureheads. "He doesn't hit the ball hard enough, isn't tall enough to develop a powerful serve and will never have the reach to play a good net game."

Dr. Bartosh laughed in their faces and worked even harder with me to improve my strokes and tactics.

"The important thing is not to miss the ball," she would tell me. "Tennis matches are won on mistakes. Let the other fellow hit the ball too hard. Let the other fellow hit the ball into the net. Let the other fellow make the mistakes. It's not how hard you hit the ball but *where* you hit it."

My build and physical equipment were suited to this type of game. I was agile and fast; it was pretty hard to hit the ball to a spot where I couldn't get to it and hit it back. I was like a good major-league shortstop. I rarely missed any ball I could get to, and I got to most of them.

With Dr. Bartosh's help and inspiration, I was developing a retrieving game based on complete court coverage, running down every ball and everlastingly keeping the ball in play.

49

For many years, I had a close relationship with Dr. Bartosh and her husband, Dr. Gerald Bartosh, who was also a fine player. They had no children and I was like one of their family. During my formative adolescent years, she molded my philosophy of tennis and emphasized good sportsmanship. Dr. Bartosh and I have remained friends, and I drop in to see her frequently at the convalescent home where she now lives. She was unquestionably the greatest single influence in my tennis career, and I have a great affection for her.

After I was already an accomplished player and ranked among the first ten, I went to Eleanor (Teach) Tennant, a colorful instructor who had developed Alice Marble and other outstanding California players. She helped me with tactics and strategy, but the basics of tennis I learned from Dr. Bartosh.

I was the best player for my age, at thirteen and fourteen, in Southern California, and Dr. Bartosh decided it was time for me to expand outside the LA area. She put in my entry for the California State Boys' Championships, at Berkeley, across the bay from San Francisco. But she fell ill just before the tournament was scheduled to start and couldn't drive me up.

My brother John, who was just as interested in my progress as Dr. Bartosh, suggested, "Let's hitchhike to Berkeley—I've got five bucks I've been saving. That ought to get us there."

I was only fourteen, but John was nine years older, so my parents reluctantly gave us permission for the thumb tour up the coast, after making arrangements for us to stay with a minister in the local Church of Christ. The trip to Berkeley was a complete success. I won the tournament, thus becoming the boy champion of California. My host also baptized me into the church, in a rite of complete submersion before the entire congregation. I've never regretted this step; I only regret that I haven't been a better church member and a better Christian through the years.

On the strength of my new title, Dr. Bartosh argued the tennis association into giving me a couple of hundred dollars in expense money for the long trip to Culver, Indiana, where the U.S. Lawn Tennis Association staged the National Boys' Championships in those days. She and I took off in a Ford for Culver, which was a long, dusty trip in 1932. On the way, Dr. Bartosh let me take the wheel and taught me to drive.

This was my first national tournament, and I was desperately eager to do well. I got as far as the semifinals, where a kid a foot taller, Don Levens, put me out. I had never been so disappointed over a loss in my life. I actually hid in a corner to try to keep from crying.

Dr. Bartosh was furious.

"The first thing you've got to learn is to be a good loser as well as a good winner," she scolded me. "When you lose, you've got to smile and congratulate your opponent. That's just good manners."

It was a tough lesson to learn but I never forgot it. She also taught me to take line calls as they came, the good with the bad, and never to argue with a linesman or umpire over whether a ball was in or out. That was another lesson I took to heart, and in the years to come I accepted bad calls as part of the game, like sun in your eyes or a windy day. I never let such a call, no matter how crucial the point, rob me of my concentration or upset me.

All the time I was playing in the Southern California boys' tournaments and traveling on occasion to sectional and national events, I was also the number-one player on the Franklin High School tennis team in LA.

I was undefeated in four years of high school dual competition. I won the California State High School singles championship three years in a row, retiring a trophy that had been in competition for a long time and which was engraved with the names of Ellsworth Vines and a lot of other famous players. Jack Kramer, who is three years younger than I, later won the trophy twice, but no one has ever won it three times.

About the time I turned sixteen and entered the ranks of junior players, a tough division that took in everyone eighteen and under, I decided I was going to devote myself completely to the game and become the world's best player. I dreamed about it one night. I saw myself playing on the center court at Wimbledon in front of a packed gallery of 16,000 people, with both the King and the Queen in the royal box. I don't know who my opponent was—someone like Bill Tilden or Don Budge. I recall vividly seeing myself run to the right side of the court and hit a forehand on the run which brought up a puff of white chalk as it caught the sideline for a winner. Then I saw myself hitting a similar sensational shot down the backhand alley for match point, jumping the net, shaking hands with my opponent, whoever he was, and accepting the applause of the crowd—and the King and Queen—as champion of the world.

After I woke up, the dream stayed with me. I knew, deep down, that some day I'd make it come true. I had absolute confidence in myself and my ability to improve my game, to rise to any situation.

At age seventeen, I developed a keen personal rivalry with Joe Hunt, who was a typical California-style serve-and-volley player. (Joe later became national singles champion in 1943 and died in a Navy training plane during the war.) I played seventeen finals in tournament competition against Joe and won all of them. The biggest victory over Joe came in the National Junior Championships at Culver, where I won my first national singles title in 1935.

That title impressed a lot of people, certainly myself and my friends and family. But not Perry Jones.

During the tournament at Culver, a wealthy tennis enthusiast from Southern California gave me added inspiration by informing me that he intended to pay all expenses for the winner of the Junior Championship to go to Wimbledon and play in the men's singles.

"I'd like to see you win it, Bobby," this gentleman said. "I'm sure it would be a wonderful experience for you, at your age."

As soon as I won the title, I sought out my wealthy friend. But he had bad news.

"I'm sorry, Bobby," he said. "The Southern California Association has wired me to call off the Wimbledon trip. I don't like to argue with those boys."

I was crushed. It was clear to me that Jones and

his cronies had changed their minds about allowing the U.S. junior champion to play at Wimbledon when they found out his name was Bobby Riggs instead of Joe Hunt. It was just one more item in a long and ever-growing list of hostile actions that soured my relations with the amateur nabobs in California.

When I turned eighteen, I decided to move on to the big-time tournaments in the East, particularly the grass-court circuit—then consisting of Longwood, Seabright, Rye, Southampton and Newport—leading up to the U.S. Nationals at Forest Hills. It was true that most of the leading players learned their tennis in California, but it was only in the major tournaments of the East that they could make their reputations.

Naturally Perry Jones flatly opposed my idea. When I asked him for expense money and official sponsorship to facilitate my entry into eastern tournaments, he told me, "You're only eighteen. You're not ready for the eastern circuit. You wouldn't do well. Besides, we want you in our junior tournaments here. Go back to Culver and defend your national junior title."

"But I've already won the junior title," I argued. "It won't prove anything for me to win it again. I want to go on to something bigger."

The argument ended with Jones telling me, "If you don't defend your junior title, you will get no official sanction and no financial help from us.

"If you go east," he emphasized, "you'll be strictly on your own. You won't be considered a representative of the Southern California Association in any way."

The door had scarcely closed behind me when Jones shot off a letter to the head office of the USLTA in New York. Jones branded me as a headstrong, rebellious junior who was defying his association and who should be shown no special consideration as national junior champion when it came to entering men's singles events.

But what Jones didn't know was that I had anticipated his reaction and had already made plans for a private tour of the eastern summer circuit. Wayne Sabin, a leading West Coast player from Oregon, had agreed to go along as my doubles partner. Most important, I had found my own sponsor for the trip. He was Jack Del Valle, a colorful guy who enjoyed betting on tennis as much as I did. He had enough money to spend most of his time at the LA Tennis Club, playing his own brand of tennis and taking the action on the frequent money matches between the better players.

Jack was something of a hero worshiper and liked to hang around sports figures. He had once managed prize fighters, he claimed, "and now I'm going to manage you two."

The three of us made quite an impression as we descended on the tennis circuit in Jack's Cadillac. Nobody had ever heard of a tennis player having his own manager. (Later the title changed to bookmaker, as Jack wandered around the courts, taking the action on our matches.) Wayne and I had designed a kind of uniform for our doubles team, a pair of mess jackets that we wore onto the court and around the clubhouses. It added to the reputation we were fast acquiring as a couple of hotshots from California, conning the effete easterners.

That reputation spread quickly along the circuit after our debut in the first tournament, the Heart of America in Kansas City. With Jack busily booking the action on our matches, I won the singles title, and Wayne and I honored our team uniforms by winning the doubles as well.

The next stop was Chicago and our first brush with the big leaguers, in the National Clay Courts Championships. The action off the court was also big league, and Jack was the busiest man in Chicago as he negotiated the odds and collected the winnings on my matches. To the astonishment of practically everybody but myself, I got to the finals against Frankie Parker, who was top seeded, and wiped him out in straight sets. Once again, Wayne and I made off with the doubles title as well. Those twin victories established me as a top contender along the circuit. Perry Jones must have been squirming back in California when he read about it. Despite his letter warning the top brass against Bobby Riggs, every tournament chairman in the country was now begging for my entry.

I now learned about the expenses racket and how it worked behind the hypocritical front put up by amateur officials. Once I got into the ranks of the top ten, I never had a problem supporting myself—and for two years a wife and child—as a so-called amateur player. Tournament chairmen would bid against each other for my services. I can remember being paid $500 cash, plus full accommodations, hotel and meals, and transportation to a small tournament in Neenah, Wisconsin, as far back as 1937. Sometimes a chairman who was trying to stay technically within the rules would bet me $100 I couldn't jump over the tennis net two or three times in a row. I never lost any of those bets.

For years I was on the personal payroll of Edmund C. Lynch, of Merrill Lynch, Pierce, Fenner & Beane—also known in Wall Street as "We the People." Mr. Lynch took a great liking to me during my early years on the eastern grass-court circuit. Somebody told him about my hassles with Perry Jones and the USLTA, who were always curious about my sub-rosa income sources. They often had me on the carpet to explain (or deny) the payoffs being made to me by their own tournament chairmen. Mr. Lynch wanted to help me financially so that I would have some independence. He also liked me to play tennis with him and his friends on his estates in Southampton on Long Island, Indian Creek in Miami, and Nassau. He traveled everywhere in his private yacht. Whenever I played at Newport, I stayed aboard the boat in Narragansett Bay. I received a check for $200 every week for two years from Mr. Lynch, until his untimely death aboard a steamship on his way to Europe.

I also had a long-standing arrangement with L. B. Icely, president of the Wilson Sporting Goods Company in Chicago. He induced me to move from Los Angeles to Chicago. He wanted to get me out of the clutches of Perry Jones and his sycophants and also wanted to boost the prestige of the Western Tennis Association, which had not boasted a top-ten player since George Lott back in the twenties.

"As the president of a big corporation, it would not be ethical for me to make under-the-table payments to you," Mr. Icely explained. "So I'm going to arrange a job for you with the United States Advertising Corporation, which handles the Wilson advertising account."

I went on the U.S. Advertising Corporation payroll at $200 a week, theoretically working on the Red Heart Dog Food account but getting all the time off I needed to play tournaments.

The watchdogs of the USLTA at 120 Broadway got wind of this arrangement somehow, and Mr. Icely decided to transfer me to another job. This turned out to be the position of assistant public-relations director of a small southern college, where I also helped coach the tennis team. The president of the college ran a publishing business on the side which did all the printing of manuals and catalogues for a major sporting goods manufacturer.

For a while there I was collecting my $200 each week and making as much as $500 in expenses from tournaments. I drove a snazzy Cord convertible, one of the first cars with front-wheel drive, stayed at the best hotels and rarely saw a bill for room or board.

The Riggs watchers at 120 Broadway eventually caught up with the college dodge and invited me to explain my PR job there and how much work I actually did.

It so happened that I had made an arrangement with a member of the Southern Tennis Association to handle all my expense checks that winter on the southern circuit. Whenever I played in a tournament, I would tell the committee to mail my expense check to this individual, hoping in that way to take some of the heat off me at 120 Broadway. I lived off my two $200 checks as I traveled through the South.

But when I got back from the Sugar Bowl Invitation Tournament, I went to the official who had been banking my checks—I thought. He had disappeared along with my checks.

When I told the members of the USLTA Rules Committee my story—which happened to be truth, not fiction, for a change—they reacted in typical fashion.

"Just keep quiet about the whole thing," they told me. "If you don't pop off about it, we won't prefer charges of professionalism against you." They never made an effort to locate the missing tennis-association official, to take any action against him or to recover my money.

The whole thing sickened but didn't surprise me. I never ceased to marvel at the hypocrisy of the top tennis officials. I hope things have improved in their ranks since they made tennis players honest in 1968 by approving open tournaments between amateurs and professionals. But I can't help having my doubts. A badge wearer is usually some guy who gets his kicks by running around a tournament looking important and whose only claim to fame is his membership in the USLTA. There are exceptions, of course, lots of dedicated people trying to do a good job for tennis. But I never met too many of them during my years of guerrilla warfare with that organization.

My experience with the U.S. Davis Cup team

would fill a whole book. The same kind of thinking that permitted the rules committee to punish players who took cash under the table but exonerated the tournament officials who paid them off seemed to prevail among the Davis Cup committeemen.

Despite the fact that I could knock off all the members of their cup teams, with the sole exception of Don Budge, the country's number-one singles player, I was not named to the team—not even when I was the second-ranking player in the country, behind Budge. One year the brass went so far as to allow me to practice with the team at Forest Hills, prior to its departure for England, but they didn't put me on the squad until Don Budge was about to turn pro in 1938.

Even then, I'm sure that some officials didn't want the Bad Boy of Tennis, as the newspapers used to call me, on their cup team. I don't know how much influence Perry Jones had with the cup committee, but I am sure he agreed with their decision not to name me to the squad until it was too embarrassing to leave me off. Jones was capable of some pretty petty behavior. One year I refused to play in Jones's pet tournament, the Pacific Southwest Championships, held in his personal bailiwick, the Los Angeles Tennis Club. Jones left word at the gate that if I showed up I would have to pay my way in. I never showed up, being too busy playing somewhere else for bigger expenses than Jones ever paid me. However, he managed to pay his top performers under the table too, just like every other tournament chairman.

I was a member of the U.S. Davis Cup teams of 1938 and 1939. We played Australia both years in the challenge round at the Merion Cricket Club in Philadelphia. In 1938, playing the singles along with Don Budge, I provided the margin of victory for the United States by beating Adrian Quist in four sets. The next year at Merion I won my opening singles against John Bromwich in three straight sets but lost to Quist in five sets on the final day. That squared the challenge round at two matches apiece, and Bromwich went on to beat Frank Parker in straight sets for an Australian victory. World War II broke out a few days later, and the Aussies took the cup home with them for the duration, just as they had in 1914 at the outbreak of World War I. I never played cup tennis again, since I was a professional by the time the competition was revived in 1946.

That first year on the eastern circuit with Sabin and our bookmaker-manager Jack Del Valle was an eye-opener for me in many ways, not just learning my way around in the world of under-the-table playoffs. I had never seen a grass court before I stepped on the beautifully tended turf at the Nassau Country Club on Long Island. This was the first of the grass-court fixtures during July and August which were climaxed by the National Championships in early September, played on the grass at the West Side Tennis Club at Forest Hills.

I quickly discovered that my kind of game was ideally suited to the fast grass surface. Its speed was not unlike that of the cement courts where I had learned to play. The bounce of the ball was low, which I also liked, and my spins, chops and drop shots worked with devastating effect on grass.

I won my first grass-court tournament, the Nassau Bowl, beating Gregory Mangin, a top tenner, in the finals. Wayne and I did well in the doubles, getting to the semifinals, where we were put out by the experienced Davis Cup team of Wilmer Allison and John Van Ryn. I reached the finals of two more grass tournaments, losing to Frank Parker and Don Budge, but played disappointingly in my first attempt at Forest Hills, losing to Van Ryn in the second round.

Nevertheless I felt pretty good about my private tour. Jones had told me, "You haven't a ghost of a chance to make the first ten," but when the official rankings came out for that year, I was placed number four among the men, although I was still a junior player.

At Forest Hills, where the newspapermen regarded me as good copy because of my betting and my running feud with the tennis brass, I had announced my five-year plan.

This called for me to make the top ten in 1936, improve my ranking in 1937, play Davis Cup tennis in 1938, win the National Championships in 1939 and become world champion after that. As it turned out, I actually accomplished all this in four years.

The year 1939, when I turned twenty-one, was my biggest year as an amateur. Don Budge had just turned pro, which automatically elevated me to his spot as number-one player in the country. The USLTA had no choice but to send me to Europe as part of their official team for the French championships and the grass-court events in England leading up to Wimbledon.

The fleshpots of Paris proved more fascinating to me than the competition in the French championships at the Roland Garros courts, which are slow clay and supposedly made to order for my type of retrieving game. But the champagne parties and the mademoiselles took my mind off tennis. I was also in the midst of a bad patch of racket trouble. I just couldn't find a racket with the right kind of feel.

During the French championships I borrowed a racket from a different player every day. Somehow I managed to reach the finals in singles against Don McNeill. I played Don using a monster of a racket, with a five-inch handle, that I had borrowed from an Irish player, George Littleton-Rogers. Don played first-rate tennis and clobbered me in the final. That night I went to the Folies Bergère for a final fling at Paris night life and got it out of my system.

When we crossed the Channel to England, I was in a serious frame of mind. But in the Queens Club tournament, the final warm-up for Wimbledon, I was still plagued by racket problems.

Besides, I was not too keen to win a tournament just before the big one. I was afraid it would be the kiss of death for me. Anyhow I got to the finals against Baron Gottfried von Cram, the great German player. I had twelve rackets on the court. He took the first set 6 to 0 and led 5 to 0 in the second. By that time I had used eleven of the rackets, changing them after every game. I finally won the twelfth game and said to myself, "This is the racket I'm going to use at Wimbledon." It was a European make, Prosser, and I later had six of them made up for me.

Von Cram went through me easily at Queens but was summoned home because of the threatening war situation on the Continent. So although it was my first Wimbledon, I was seeded number one in the men's singles, not on my recent showings abroad but because of my U.S. ranking. Knowing my liking for betting action, the London newspapers accused me of deliberately losing to von Cram in order to lower the odds on myself at Wimbledon. This was not true. But I must admit that the first thing I did after Queens was to seek out one of the legal bookmaking shops in London. John Olliff, an English player, took me along to his favorite bookmaker.

"What are the odds on Riggs to win the men's singles?" I asked. Three to one, was the reply. I protested that the price ought to be higher on a guy making his first bid for the Wimbledon title, but the bookmaker was firm. I put down a hundred pounds on myself in the singles. The pound was worth about five U.S. dollars at that time.

I then told the bookie that if I won the singles I'd let the money go on myself in the doubles.

Olliff, who was fond of me and acting as my adviser, exclaimed, "How can you do that, Bobby? If you win the singles, that will be fantastic on your first try," he pointed out. "How can you win the doubles too? You and your partner [Elwood Cooke] were beaten in the semis at Paris by two old men, Borotra and Brugnon."

"Then I ought to get a good price on the doubles," I replied. But the bookmaker offered me only 6 to 1 on the men's doubles—double the price of the singles.

I took the odds but told the bookie I would have got at least 10 to 1 from an American bookmaker.

He was not impressed. He thought that was the end of the transaction.

But I said, "Well, if I get lucky and win the singles and the doubles, I might as well put it all on the mixed doubles and go for the hat trick."

Olliff exploded. "You're out of your mind," he told me. "I've met a lot of cocky kids, but you take the cake. Nobody ever won all three Wimbledon events on the first try. You'll be lucky to win the singles, much less the other two finals."

Well, I thought the odds would really go up for the mixed doubles, but the best the bookie would do was double them again. So I left the shop with a parlay of 3 to 1 on myself in the singles, 6 to 1 on the doubles and 12 to 1 on the mixed doubles riding on my original hundred pounds.

I've always believed the incentive of the parlay made the difference at Wimbledon that year. I was down two sets to one in the singles final against Cooke when I thought about my investment. That was sufficient to spur me into taking the last two sets for the singles title.

Cooke was my doubles partner, and we survived a few rough spots to get to the final in that event, breezing past Charlie Hare and Frank Wilde of England in straight sets. Two down and one to go.

In my final hurdle, the mixed doubles, I was fortunate to be paired with Alice Marble—who had also won the singles title and the women's doubles with Sarah Fabyan. So Alice and I were both shooting for the Triple Crown—but she didn't have what I had riding on it. We took the mixed doubles final without loss of a set.

I was at the bookmaker's shop first thing Monday morning to collect on my parlay. It added up to £21,600, the equivalent of $108,000. That was the biggest bet I ever won on myself in tennis, before or since.

As an amateur in good, if shaky, standing with my association, I was afraid to open up a bank account with the money. I stashed it away in a London bank vault, intending to get it out the following year. But war broke out the next month, and wartime restrictions prevented me from getting my pounds out of the safe-deposit box. If they had been in a bank account I could have transferred the money to the United States. So I had my own special reasons—108,000 of them—for wanting to see Hitler lose the war. I sweated out the Battle of Britain from a distance and nobody rooted harder than I did for the RAF to halt the German invasion of England.

I capped my Wimbledon victory two months later that year at Forest Hills by taking the U.S. singles title as well.

I was twenty-one years of age, the number-one amateur player in the world, and looking for other worlds to conquer. But Don Budge, Ellsworth Vines and Fred Perry were dominating the pro touring scene and there was no room for me in their league yet. I hoped to be ready the next year.

In the meantime, I wasn't too unhappy about remaining amateur. Because 1939 was notable in my private life too. I married beautiful blonde Kay Fischer of Chicago, where I had been living for two years, ever since going on the Wilson Sporting Goods payroll. We were married in early December—during the Chicago Indoor City Championships. Our honeymoon night was spent in the Palmer House. I had to be at the courts bright and early next day to practice for what turned out to be quite a day's—and night's—work, no less than fifteen sets of tennis!

I played five sets with Jimmy Evert—now famous as the father of teen-age marvel Chris Evert—to win the singles final. I then teamed with Frank Froehling (father of the player presently touring with World Championship Tennis), who had been best man at my wedding, to win the doubles final, also in five sets. After that I played a two-set mixed doubles semifinal and won that final, with Helen Fulton Shockley, in three tough sets.

For Kay, it was quite an introduction to married life with a tennis player. She watched every one of my matches huddled in a fur coat in the cold Chicago armory. But later on we had a real honeymoon on the southern tennis circuit, where I was able to loaf through early round matches and pay more attention to my lovely young wife.

My dream of joining the pro tour was shattered the next year at Forest Hills, where I had hoped to defend my national title successfully and sign a contract for a $25,000 professional guarantee, a substantial sum those days in sport.

I met Don McNeill in the final and took the first two sets easily—too easily. I could see dollar signs before my eyes. My concentration wandered and I let Don, a tough, resourceful fighter, back into the match. He tied it at two sets all. I've never tried harder to win than I did in that long fifth set, but Don finally took it 7 to 5.

Without the Forest Hills title I lacked the drawing power needed on the pro tour, and I resigned myself to another year in amateur ranks. Kay and I and our infant son, Bobby, Jr., were living well, what with my income from Wilson and the large tournament expenses I was now able to command.

My principal aim was to recover the U.S. championship. I went into serious training and dieting, with Kay's help, to get myself into perfect physical shape. My nemesis in that comeback year was not McNeill but Frank Kovacs, the Clown Prince of Tennis, a likable screwball with a tremendous tennis game. Kovacs was the master psycher of all time and he pulled every trick in the book—and devised a few new ones—in the ten matches we played before Forest Hills. He stalled on changeovers, staged sit-down strikes on the court in protest over line calls and hammed it up for the galleries, who loved all his antics. One time I came out for a match in shorts while Frankie wore the traditional long white flannels. He kept pointing to my shorts and laughing. Finally he produced a pair of scissors and cut his flannels off above the knees.

"You haven't got a thing on me now, Riggs," he shouted.

By that time my concentration and my patience were both used up, and Kovacs walked off with the match.

Kovacs and I were tied at four matches apiece at the end of the southern circuit in the spring of 1941. He was secretly married to another tournament player, Virginia Wolfenden, and I beat the bridegroom in our next two encounters on the grass-court circuit. I was certain that it was going to be Kovacs, not defending champion Don McNeill, whom I would have to subdue for the title that meant so much to me.

That's the way it turned out. Kovacs whipped McNeill soundly in the semifinals at Forest Hills, as I beat Ted Schroeder to reach the final and what I regarded as the most important match of my life, with my future at stake. Kovacs was favored to beat me at odds of 2 to 1—at least that's what I got when I backed myself with all my loose cash.

Frankie took the opening set 7 to 5, but I wasn't upset. I was so fit and strong that I knew I could go five sets at top speed if necessary. I took the next two sets easily and was in full command of the match. The last thing I wanted was to let Kovacs talk to his coach, George Hudson, during the intermission and change his tactics.

At the end of the third set, Kovacs slumped into a chair alongside the umpire's stand and picked up a cold drink.

"You look tired, Frankie," I told him, as I toweled myself. "I guess you want to go in and lie down awhile."

Frankie flared up. "Who's tired? Not me. Let's go out there and finish this." I had outpsyched the master psycher.

So we told the umpire we wanted to skip the

traditional ten-minute rest period. We went right back on the court, and my momentum carried me through a 6-to-3 fourth set for the match and the all-important national championship.

Soon afterward I signed a pro contract for $25,000 with Lex Thompson, the young millionaire sportsman who owned the Philadelphia Eagles football team. He put together a tour featuring Don Budge, Fred Perry, Frank Kovacs (whose clowning was considered good box office in the pro ranks) and me.

I left the amateur ranks with relief, free forever of phony shamateurism and the scrutiny of the Riggs watchers at 120 Broadway. I was an honest tennis player at last.

3

My first pro tour was doomed before it got started. We opened at Madison Square Garden on December 26, 1941—nineteen days after the Japs bombed Pearl Harbor and took people's minds off such things as indoor tennis. Promoter Lex Thompson had to give away thousands of dollars' worth of tickets to taxi drivers and bellhops in order to fill the seats for our New York debut.

Other troubles quickly followed. During the third set of my match, Fred Perry fell and hurt his elbow so badly he had to be carried to the nearest hospital.

Perry was replaced in the tour by Gene Mako and then by Lester Stoefen, who lacked the star quality of Perry. Attendances got smaller as we went along. Wartime shortages plagued us. We couldn't get tires for our cars and trucks, and people stayed home because gasoline was rationed. Thompson called the tour off after we had played seventy out of ninety scheduled dates. He took a financial beating but paid us our guarantees, like a true sportsman.

When the tour ended, Don Budge was on top, with most matches won. I was in second place. I realized that whenever the war ended and pro tennis resumed, Budge was the man I would have to contend with.

This conviction grew when Budge beat me decisively in the finals of the U.S. Professional Championships at Forest Hills in 1942. That was my last big match before I received the President's Greetings and entered boot camp at Great Lakes Naval Training Station.

I cut a pretty ludicrous figure in bell-bottom trousers, and the drudgery of Navy training was a great contrast to the free-and-easy life I had recently been enjoying on the proceeds of our tennis tour. But I can't complain about my two years in the U.S. Navy. As a well-known athlete, I was quickly assigned to Commander Gene Tunney's training school at Bainbridge, Maryland, along with Johnny Mize, Peewee Reese, Johnny Rigney and other sports celebrities, and eventually became a specialist first class.

I shipped out for Pearl Harbor on the cruiser *Birmingham* and made $500 en route playing poker with baseball players Skeets Dickey, Johnny Lucadello, Buddy Blattner and other shipmates. Added to the money I had made shooting crap at specialists' school in Bainbridge, this gave me a very nice nest egg. I used a thousand dollars of it for a secondhand Cadillac, which the Navy okayed for me to buy in Hawaii, to get around to the tennis exhibitions and clinics I staged for servicemen.

I went on a long tour of Pacific outposts with a

group of baseball players. They played exhibition games, and afterward I played exhibition tennis matches with Peewee Reese acting as ball boy and Johnny Rigney doing the umpiring.

Then I settled down for the duration on the island of Guam, where Vice Admiral John Hoover, a keen tennis enthusiast, had ordered the Seabees to build a tennis court. My most important duty on Guam was to keep a 4 P.M. tennis date with the admiral and his aides. We played doubles. Of course I was the admiral's partner.

But Guam also gave me a chance to practice serious tennis, in preparation for the day I would take on Budge again. My old touring pal, Wayne Sabin, was also in the Navy. He was stationed on Guam for a while, and we played a lot of close matches. I often wondered whether Budge, then an Army Air Corps lieutenant stationed in Arizona, was working on his game as hard as I was. I had a chance to find out, when Admiral Hoover and his aides decided to stage a series of Davis Cup-style matches between two-man teams representing the Army and Navy.

Sabin and I represented the Navy, and Budge and Parker played for the Army. The matches were played at various Pacific bases and proved highly popular. We drew big crowds of servicemen, and there was plenty of action—on and off the courts. For me, the most fascinating thing about the series was the opportunity to play Budge, who was three years older than I and had always been able to beat me, both in the amateur and professional ranks.

Budge and I split our first four interservice

matches, and our final meeting took place on the island of Tinian.

"If I beat Don today," I told Sabin, "I'll know for sure I can handle him from now on."

The match was a tense, seesaw affair. We split the first two sets, and I won the third 8 to 6. I was elated. I was sure that I could overcome Budge, who represented the last obstacle to my becoming world champion, come V-Day.

Soon after that happy day arrived, I was shipped back to San Francisco, where I shared a thirty-day leave with Kay and our two young sons, Bobby, Jr., and Larry. But before the leave was up I was playing tennis again, which hardly came as a surprise to Kay.

We moved south to the Los Angeles Tennis Club, which was coming alive again with the return of Perry, Mako, Budge, Parker, myself and others from the Pacific. We organized a series of singles and doubles matches, which were real action events. Errol Flynn, Bruce Cabot, Walter Pidgeon, Pat DiCicco and other big bettors were red-hot Budge rooters. Mervyn LeRoy and Ozzie Nelson always backed me—and did pretty well.

Soon after my discharge from the Navy in November 1945, Budge and I played two important matches. I beat him in the final of the World Hard Court Championships in Los Angeles, but he developed a cramp in his arm in the final set which somewhat clouded my win. His supporters, notably Flynn and DiCicco, then organized a showdown challenge match between Budge and myself in the Pan-Pacific Auditorium in Los Angeles. The two organizers made a series of heavy bets, including one with me, on their tall red-haired hero.

The match was close. Budge got off to a fast start, taking the first set 6 to 4 and opening up a 5-to-2 lead in the second. By dint of all-out scampering I won that set 9 to 7 and took the third 6 to 4, Don had set points in the fourth set but I finally took it 8 to 6 for the match, $3,300 in prize money and a considerable sum I was happy to collect from Messrs. Flynn and DiCicco.

With those two victories, plus the wins I had over him in the Pacific, I gained complete mastery over Budge. I was still in my twenties and at the peak of my ability. Budge had turned thirty and had lost something of the greatness he had possessed before the war. I think he was less daring. He got smarter as he got older. He was more cautious and quit taking chances. When he was younger, he was reckless. He took chances—but made them all. He had great shots. But after the war he took something off the ball and played his shots safer. I could play against that kind of game.

Budge and I made two world tours, in 1946 and 1947, and I won both of them. They were only moderately successful financially, since pro tennis was more or less in the doldrums. The eyes of the tennis world were then focused on young Jack Kramer, who was burning up the amateur courts with a series of great wins at Wimbledon and Forest Hills.

It was obvious that Kramer would be the next great pro star, and his first tour would make a fortune for all concerned. His would be the first new face on the pro tour since mine, five years earlier. And Jack had the big game, the serve-and-volley attack with sound ground strokes to go with it.

Naturally, in light of two years of fairly constant wins over Budge, I thought of myself as the obvious opponent for Kramer. But Jack Harris, who was then promoting the tour, was a lifelong supporter of Budge. To him, my long series of victories over Budge was some kind of fluke. He still felt Budge was the better player—and the better box-office attraction.

Harris let it be known that the winner of the 1947 Professional Championships at Forest Hills would get the $100,000 plum, the chance to meet Kramer on the next tour. Kramer was set to turn pro after the U.S. Nationals later that summer, win or lose. As it happened, he won it, adding even more luster to his name and to his box-office appeal.

So Budge got a chance to reinstate himself as the top professional in a single tournament which would wipe out all the defeats of the two past years. I didn't see the justice of this, but arguing with Harris got me nowhere. I had to prove myself all over again, on the basis of one tournament at Forest Hills. I had the feeling that I was going to have a rough few days on the grass, even though it was my favorite surface.

I was right. Frank Kovacs, who always gave me trouble, had been playing great tennis all year. He told everyone that he had finally found his touch and was a sure thing to sweep the courts at Forest Hills. I met Kovacs in the semifinals and beat him in straight sets, but the match drained a lot of my energy, mental and physical.

I felt flat and lethargic when I came out for the all-important final with Budge. We were nervous and tentative, both of us thinking about the potential

$100,000 contract and unwilling to take chances with that much at stake. The temperature was a blazing 95 degrees. It was not a day for high-caliber tennis.

I got out to a lead, two sets to one, but Budge deuced the match in a fast-paced fourth set. We both suffered from cramps in the final set, which I finally took 6 to 3 after Don saved three match points. I thought that we had played mediocre tennis, but Sabin disagreed.

"It was a great match," he reassured me. "Pressure tennis all the way. It was damned interesting."

So when Jack Kramer turned pro following his five-set final victory over Frankie Parker at Forest Hills, I was waiting for him. Kramer, three years my junior, was being touted in the press as one of the all-time greats, but I was confident that I could defend my world championship against him.

The night Jack Kramer made his professional debut against me in Madison Square Garden was a night to remember for many reasons, not the least of which was the weather. It was the day after Christmas, December 26, 1947, and the biggest blizzard in years had struck the New York area. More than two feet of snow paralyzed transportation, stranding buses, taxicabs and private cars in the middle of streets and in the highways leading in and out of the city. We thought we had a financial disaster on our hands, but we underestimated the incredible public interest in our match.

Jack had won Wimbledon and Forest Hills, was the premier exponent of the big game and widely regarded as unbeatable. I was the professional champion, who had beaten Don Budge and everyone else on the pro tour. My much greater experience was supposed to give me the edge, particularly under the lights and the trying conditions of indoor competition.

As a result of the wide-scale speculation over the match, 15,114 people trudged to the Garden through the snow, some of them on snowshoes and skis. How they all got there I'll never know, but they came from near and far, a lot of them willing to back their hero, Kramer, with hard cash.

I spent a busy hour or so before the match, making bets on myself with the Kramer fans. At the start of play I was still negotiating at courtside, but then I settled down to concentrate on the tactics I had worked out in advance.

Jack was supposed to be the net rusher and I was supposed to be the retriever. But I fooled everybody, including Kramer, by racing to the net behind everything. This put Jack off balance and he was never able to hit his stride. I also lobbed into the lights all night long. Jack later learned to handle my lobs with ease, but on this occasion he was helpless against them. I won that first match and about $5,000 in bets.

After opening night in the Garden I forgot about betting, though. Just playing Jack was incentive enough for me. It was a terrific series of battles. The first twenty-five matches took us about two months. We played a match every two or three days, traveling constantly between cities three or four hundred miles apart. In addition to playing we had to do an active job of selling tickets to each match, through publicity dates and interviews in department stores and radio and TV stations. It was a real grind. I had gone through it before but never with Jack Kramer.

He had the advantage of playing his natural serve-and-volley game. The only defense against him, as I showed in the initial match at the Garden, was to take the net myself. But whereas Jack had played the serve-volley game from the time he was a boy champion, I was more like Bitsy Grant, Frank Parker, Pancho Segura and later Ken Rosewall. We were all originally baseliners who had to learn how to volley and play the net.

Luckily I had a very good serve, a deceptive one that I could place well to the forehand or backhand. I was able to outace Kramer on the tour, just as I out-aced other big servers such as Gonzales. I was quick and agile on returning, so that I got a lot of balls back which might have been aces against other players.

The stakes were high for me in the Kramer series. I realized that the survivor would get to play the next amateur champion to turn pro, while the loser would be dropped from the tour, just as Budge had been dropped when I beat him.

All things considered, I did well against Kramer at the beginning of the tour. He had a margin of one match over me, 13 to 12, at the end of twenty-five matches, and he led 16 to 14 at the end of thirty matches. But then he broke loose from me. I began to tire. Playing Kramer night after night was like pitching a World Series game. My arm began to wear out from the constant serving and volleying at maximum speed and power. Kramer was bigger and stronger and gaining in confidence all the time.

Jack had a natural rhythm on his serve, with a great big arc to his motion. His first serve was almost the equal of a Gonzales or Vines delivery. But Kramer was in a class by himself when it came to the second serve, which was almost as tough as his first ball. So even if he faulted his first serve, which was not often, I was faced with returning a ball that was nearly as difficult to handle.

I used the lob more against Jack than ever—fifty or sixty times a match—to keep him from crowding the net. But I'd have to spin a perfect high lob to the corners to beat him with that shot. I can't remember him missing a single smash in the hundred matches we played. That's how fantastic he was overhead.

Jack was utterly relentless in his savage attacking game. Sometimes we played until one o'clock in the morning—there were no tie breakers in those days. We would play sets that went 14 to 12. It was brutal. The pace of the matches and the strain of constant traveling, the grind of one-night stands, wore me down to the point where I got a bad cold. In Fort Worth I ran a 102-degree fever and should have stayed in bed. But the promoter said, rightly, that the show must go on. I lost that night 6–0, 6–0.

That score proves that pro tennis was on the up and up, despite the contention of cynics who claimed our matches were fixed. Even though Jack had built up a big lead over me in our series, he refused to give me a single break when he had me at his mercy. It was a lousy match from the spectators' viewpoint, but Jack didn't try to make it look good. He wouldn't throw a point or a game. The people in Fort Worth were sour on pro tennis for years after that night.

I never threw a match in pro tennis and I don't know any player who did. The setup was absolutely honest. There was no organized gambling on tennis, no mutuels, no Las Vegas line, no bookmakers. There was plenty of so-called friendly betting among spectators, as I have good reason to know. But players never bet with each other. There was no way any pro was going to let another pro beat him in those days.

I believe it is the same with the players on the WCT tour now, although they don't have the enormous pressure to win that we always felt. Nowadays the pros are guaranteed an annual salary of $12,000 a year by Lamar Hunt, whether they earn it or not. But the incentive at the top, where a $50,000 top prize is now possible in a single playoff, makes it inconceivable that players of the stature of Stan Smith, Rod Laver, Ken Rosewall, Arthur Ashe and the rest would ever dream of throwing a match. Those who talk glibly of crooked matches have no conception of the tremendous pride every pro takes in his game and in every performance.

Kramer kept the pressure on me in every match, even when he was far ahead. On the odd occasion he lost, he was furious with himself. He was a merciless competitor and possessed the killer instinct in the highest degree. He always gave his best. He fought from the first match to the last in our series and beat me by a final margin of three to one. It was one of the finest exhibitions of sustained tennis brilliance in the history of the game.

If I had to lose my world championship, I was not sorry about losing it to Jack Kramer, who went on to beat Pancho Segura, Frank Sedgman and Pancho Gonzales in other tours and eventually retire undefeated.

That grueling tour against Kramer convinced me that there had to be an easier way to earn a living. I had no desire to take second place on a tour with Kramer playing the next amateur to turn pro. I had been champion too long, number one in the world, and my pride—ego, if you will—wouldn't let me sign up for another tour in a minor role.

As it happened, Kramer was dissatisfied with the way Jack Harris had set up our tour, although it was a great success financially, particularly for Kramer. So Jack said to me, "We don't need Harris. Why don't you take over from him? You'd make a terrific promoter."

This sounded good to me. My ego was bruised by the beating I had taken from Kramer, and I was looking for some way to remain in tennis without being number two or worse.

The idea of being the big promoter, cigar in my mouth, wheeling and dealing, talking to the press, appealed to me. As it turned out, I proved to be a natural at the business.

My first promotion was supposed to be Kramer versus Ted Schroeder, a tenacious, crowd-pleasing Californian who seemed to specialize in coming from behind in five-set matches. He was a great pal of Kramer's. When Schroeder beat Jaroslav Drobny (in five sets) to win Wimbledon in 1949, he was the hottest amateur in the world. Kramer was there and got

Schroeder's signature on a professional contract, to go into effect after the Forest Hills championships that year.

But Schroeder got cold feet after he got back home and pulled out of the deal. I was glad to see him go down to Gonzales in five sets at Forest Hills, after he had ruined the tour we had set up.

Kramer said, "The hell with Schroeder, let's get Gonzales instead." So I got on the same plane with Gonzales, returning to LA after Forest Hills, and by the time we landed I had his signature on a contract. Gonzales kept his word, and I was in business as a promoter, staging a worldwide series of matches between Gonzales and Kramer. I traveled everywhere with the players, introduced them to the audiences, booked all the arenas, handled the publicity and enjoyed myself thoroughly on the sidelines.

The tour was a financial success, and although Kramer won it by the margin of ninety-six matches to twenty-seven, Gonzales showed tremendous potential for a twenty-year-old, in his first year as a pro. Every third or fourth match Pancho would come out on the court with fire in his eye, growl, "I'm gonna win this match," and play inspirational-type tennis to beat Kramer. After that tour Gonzales retired for several years, but when he came back he proved to be a better player than ever.

With Gonzales gone, there were no particularly attractive amateurs to turn pro against Kramer. However, the newspapers were filled with pictures of Gussie Moran, wearing lace panties specially designed for her by Teddy Tenling. Gorgeous Gussie, a shapely California girl, drew so many photographers to her matches at Wimbledon in 1949 that she couldn't concentrate on the game. She was put out in an early round, to the chagrin of the male spectators, but her fame was by then worldwide.

Local arena operators all over the country were eager to put Gussie on the court. I signed her up to play against Pauline Betz on my next tour, in which Kramer was pitted against veteran pro Pancho Segura, an underrated player capable of beating anybody in the game.

I realized that Pauline was a better player than Gussie. But I wasn't prepared for Pauline trying to upstage Gussie in the glamour-panties department. But that's what happened. On opening night in Madison Square Garden, Gussie trotted out in her famous lace panties. But Pauline got louder applause when she ran into the spotlight in a pair of bright leopard-spotted shorts.

That tour, in which Kramer dominated Segura, did not do as well as the previous one, although we all made money. Gussie continued to fascinate the photographers everywhere we went, but tennis fans did not put down their money to see her play. The girls were a flop on that tour. I'm convinced it's a mistake to play men's and women's matches in the same event. The contrast between the two games is too great and reflects badly on the women. They belong on their own circuit, separated from men players, as has been shown by the success of the Virginia Slims tour. At any rate, that was the last tennis tour I promoted.

I took an unfortunate fling at a baseball promotion, pitting stars of the American League against stars of the National League. On paper it had seemed like a great idea. But after the World Series is over and the football season is under way, you can forget about exhibition baseball tours—unless you want to go to Japan. I learned this the hard way. It was a $40,000 lesson.

So I went back to tennis and started to put together what I thought was a dream promotion featuring the two big Australian Davis Cup stars, Frank Sedgman and Ken McGregor, who were still amateurs, and the two Panchos—Gonzales and Segura. But when word of this leaked Down Under, a Sydney newspaper launched a public subscription drive to give Sedgman and his bride-to-be a cash wedding gift. This was nothing more than a thinly disguised bribe to keep Frank amateur and eligible for the Davis Cup, which loomed as large then in Australian eyes as the Holy Grail. So Frank remained amateur and reneged, as did McGregor. Pancho Gonzales was also giving me a hard time, throwing a lot of last-minute demands into our contract negotiations.

At the time I was having all these troubles, I went to Florida for an exhibition match against Gar Mulloy.

I saw an attractive girl on an adjoining court at the La Gorce Country Club and asked the pro to introduce us. Her name was Priscilla Wheelan, and like myself she was in the process of getting a divorce. My marriage with Kay had gone on the rocks mainly as the result of my prolonged absences from home—two years in service during the war, and then another four or five years in which I traveled constantly either as a playing pro or as a promoter. With two youngsters to be looked after, Kay had to stay home during those years and we just drifted apart. Our divorce was friendly, and Kay took custody of the children.

As a native Californian, I had never thought much of Florida. But after I met Priscilla, who was living there in her father's home, it seemed a pleasant place. I decided to remain in Florida and abandon the promotion of the tour I had planned. I was sick of the demanding schedule of one-night stands and constant traveling all over the world. Jack Kramer took over from me as the tour promoter and made a bundle for himself—by the standards of those days. The pros today, with their million-dollar circuits and $50,000 finals, laugh at what we considered big money.

Priscilla was a wealthy girl. Her family owned the American Photograph Corporation, which does a large portrait business in department stores and in high school and college yearbooks.

For a while after we married I had a few tennis franchises going in Florida, including running the pro shop and teaching at the Roney Plaza Hotel in Miami Beach. But then I decided to go into Priscilla's family business and we moved to New York, where the company had its headquarters.

About the time I was introduced to Priscilla, I was also introduced to the game of golf. They both changed my life considerably. After being bitten by the golf bug, I got out of tennis altogether and hardly touched a racket for the next sixteen years, except for occasional friendly betting matches.

4

GOLF OPENED UP a whole new world to me. I took up the game in the period of postwar prosperity, when people had plenty of time to spend on the links and plenty of money to bet on themselves.

At the La Gorce Country Club in Miami Beach, I saw ordinary golfers shooting eighty-five and ninety and betting all kinds of money. I asked myself, "How long has this been going on?" I went out on the course and took a few shots off the first tee. I figured that anybody who was any kind of athlete at all should have no trouble playing this game. Without taking a lesson, but by watching good players carefully, I was soon breaking a hundred consistently. The game intrigued me. It was a real challenge. It wasn't long before I was shooting in the eighties. In my first year at the game I got my handicap down to sixteen. That meant that I was rated sixteen shots above par seventy-two—or eighty-eight.

Golf lends itself beautifully to betting because of

this handicapping system. According to the official rules, a handicap is determined by the average score of a player's most recent twenty rounds.

But in most friendly betting, handicaps are worked out on the first tee after a lot of arguing and negotiating. I always enjoyed the negotiating as much as I did the golf itself. Someone once said, "Golf matches are not won on the fairways or greens. They are won on the tee—the first tee." Somebody else also said, "The second worst thing in the world is betting on a golf game and losing. The worst is not betting at all." I've never agreed with any philosophy more.

I soon discovered that my lifelong competitive background in tennis was a tremendous plus factor on the golf course. If I played a businessman on vacation who had the same handicap as mine, he would fall apart when the going got tough. As soon as we had a little bet going, he would start slicing, shanking, making mistakes of all kinds. I always thrived under pressure in tennis and the same thing held true in golf, particularly when the money was down. I respond to pressure. I love it. When I'm in a tight spot, I rise to the occasion.

People called me a hustler and a thief when I was shooting to a ten handicap: "That son of a gun should be a six or eight handicap." That wasn't true. I really was a legitimate ten. But I had intangibles that made me better than another ten. This held true all the way down, as I improved and my handicap dropped to three, which was as low as it ever got—meaning that I consistently shot in the seventies.

I never did take any lessons. I just played along

with good players—occasionally with someone like Sammy Snead—and watched how they did it.

Life magazine was responsible for giving me a false reputation back in those days, one that has stayed with me. In an article entitled "Larceny on the Links" the magazine ran my picture along with those of the big hustlers of the time—John Montague, Titanic Thompson and others. They were the real thing, authentic hustlers, but I didn't belong in that company. I didn't play that well. Besides, I never falsified my handicap as most hustlers will, if given the opportunity. The only reason *Life* included me in the list was that I was a well-known figure in another sport who had turned to golf with some success.

The magazine did quote me correctly as stating that "golf courses today are just big, open-air pool-rooms" and warning unsuspecting golfers against betting with strangers on the course.

The game of golf itself is somewhat like billiards or pool, in that a great deal of manual dexterity, rather than athletic skill, is a prime requisite. Also, you are striking a ball lying still, rather than one in the air. The easy money on the links undoubtedly attracted individuals who would otherwise be hustling suckers in the poolroom.

The characters involved in golf hustling were a colorful lot, and I played against some of them in the early days of my own golf career. Martin Stanovich, better known as the Fat Man, was an overweight, awkward guy who straddled the ball and gave the impression that he was nothing but a hacker, a novice who didn't belong on the same tee with the likes of the

89

Sneads and Hogans. Many of his opponents made the mistake of jumping to that conclusion.

"Look at that guy," Lee Trevino once said. "You'd say he couldn't beat his way out of a paper bag. But he'll sixty-eight you to death—a hell of a player."

Trevino himself was a hustler as a teen-age kid, fighting his way out of the caddie yard to respectability. Lee used to bet on himself against older, better-equipped players on a par-three course in Texas. He sometimes used, as a club, a Dr. Pepper bottle wrapped with tape. He consistently shot twenty-three or twenty-four on a par-twenty-seven course and once got down as low as twenty-one, using that unorthodox weapon. (This stunt also put him on the Dr. Pepper soft-drink payroll as publicity representative.)

"My main gimmick was to bet I could beat a guy using left-handed clubs," he reminisced. "I just turned the clubs around. You can play almost as well that way as with the regular face."

Titanic Thompson, who was in his seventies when I first saw him in action, was a lean, tall guy who had a bagful of tricks as well as clubs. One of his favorite stunts was to play somebody right-handed, lose the round and then offer to play left-handed if he got a generous handicap. The stakes would increase to $5,000 or $10,000, and Titanic would win—because he was a natural southpaw.

Titanic would bet you $10,000 he could hit a golf ball a mile. Then he'd take you to the top of Pike's Peak and slam the ball downhill. Or he'd take you to a frozen lake in the wintertime and hit the ball across the ice—it would never stop.

When age began to catch up with him, Titanic collected a stable of young unknown players who shot better-than-average golf. He took them on tour and matched them against established players for big stakes. Ben Hogan was supposed to have been a member of this stable as a youngster.

Golf writer Will Grimsley tells of one of Titanic's protégés who could knock the ball a mile, hit all the greens with his approach shots and putt like Jack Nicklaus. Titanic would plant this kid in the caddie yard. After losing an eighteen-hole match, Titanic would turn to his opponent and say, "I can't beat you —but I'll bet my caddie can." The bet was immediately escalated and Titanic's caddie won his match.

In the early fifties, the rough was full of colorful characters, all looking for action. There was the Wiggler, Shaggy Ralph, the Dog Man, Charlie the Blade, Three-Iron Ward, the Fireman, Sneezy and the Whiskey Drinker, the Stork and the Invalid. There was also supposed to be a strawberry-blonde lady hustler, but I never caught up with her. This was long before the days of Women's Lib, and the golf courses I played on were a male monopoly.

Charlie the Blade used only one club, a four iron, but he could do as much with it as most pros using all fourteen clubs.

The Stork's gimmick was to play every shot off his right foot with his left stuck up behind him. He could shoot a seventy-one that way, too. The Invalid complained loudly about his aching back but always managed to beat his handicap.

The Whiskey Drinker carried a flask around the

course with him. I suspected that the flask contained nothing stronger than tea, but he started nipping on the first hole and by the time he reached the ninth tee he was lurching and "tipsy." He would demand loudly that all bets be doubled—then sober up on the back nine and take all the dough.

I saw or played against this ragtag gang, but I never met the legendary Mystery Man, John Montague, who earned his reputation in California. He was a product of the municipal golf courses but ended up playing for high stakes with Bing Crosby, Bob Hope and the Hollywood golf set. Montague was, among other things, a trick-shot artist. He once played a round in the low seventies using nothing but farming implements—a hay rake, a shovel and the like. For a bet, he once knocked a sparrow off a telephone pole with a two-iron shot. He could blast a buried ball out of a sand trap with a wooden club. He had all kinds of stunts. In a motel room he would open the window six inches and chip balls through the opening time after time without breaking the glass.

But, *Life* magazine to the contrary, I was never in a class with these authentic hustlers.

I never falsified my handicap. This is the cardinal sin in golf and one that eventually produced a major scandal.

This occurred during a so-called Calcutta-pool handicap match at the Deepdale Country Club on Long Island in 1955. I played in the match but knew nothing about the two golfers from New Jersey who won it.

Calcutta pools were declared illegal by the U.S. Golf Association after what happened at Deepdale.

Calcutta pools ran as high as $250,000 in those days. The one at Deepdale was a comparatively modest $45,000 affair. In a Calcutta, teams were auctioned off to bidders, usually club members, for prices based on the declared handicaps of the players. The two New Jersey golfers listed handicaps of seventeen and eighteen and bought tickets on themselves in the Calcutta pool. Actually their handicaps were three. So they had no trouble at all winning their match for a prize of $16,000. Someone in the crowd who knew their real handicaps recognized them and complained to the officials—after they had left with the money. In the resulting hue and cry, Calcuttas were outlawed by all golf clubs. The incident alerted the golf public to the activities of the hustlers and put most of them out of business.

Golf is a far better betting game than tennis, which is one reason I was so intrigued by it. You can handicap tennis in a lot of weird ways, as I will point out later. In golf everybody handicaps the same way, by strokes.

There are a thousand and one ways of betting on golf—and I've tried them all.

The standard bet is the Nassau. In fifty-dollar Nassaus, which were commonplace in Florida in those days, you bet fifty dollars on the first nine, fifty dollars on the second nine and fifty dollars on the lowest eighteen-hole score—for a total Nassau of one hundred fifty dollars. They tell me the average Nassau now is two dollars, which shows you what's happened in this country since those free-spending days.

In those days in Florida the money seemed to grow on the palm trees. People were playing golf every day—and playing the stock market over the phone. There were a lot of regulars on the links who were steadily betting thousand-dollar Nassaus or more on every round. They were oil millionaires from Texas and people who had cleaned up in real estate or stocks. They had money and didn't mind betting it. Of course there were the occasional sharks and hustlers. I was always careful about the people I played with. I had an occasional adventure with the sharpies but I never really got hurt. I was always pretty good about figuring a player's true handicap. Everyone knew what mine was, too.

Since I took up golf so late in life, I never developed a really good, grooved swing. I was not a long driver—225 or 230 yards or so off the tee. But I did learn to play well around the greens. I had "touch" with a golf club, just as I had with a tennis racket. I was good at chipping—using a sand wedge that Sammy Snead gave me when I first started—and became a first-class putter. I was so good that sometimes tournament players such as Gary Player and Bruce Crampton asked me how I did it. My answer probably puzzled them: "I just stare at the hole. I concentrate on getting the ball in the hole. I don't know how I do it—but it just goes in."

I've always been able to concentrate well in tight situations in golf or tennis, and that is an important factor in winning big-money matches. I've heard stories about golfers freezing on the green when faced with a big-money putt for a match. Ben Hogan, at the close of his career, was unable to move his putter back to make a shot because of this dread malady.

Down in Miami Beach I'd often play a round of golf with a half-dozen bets going with bookmakers who followed me around the course. These guys would try to distract me when I was about to make a shot. Just as I leaned over the ball, they'd crash two golf carts together. They'd move around me on the tee or the green to disturb me. But I knew what they were up to and I never let them bother me. They'd make all kinds of noise. I just played the ball.

Often these fellows did not stop at being noisy. They had all kinds of "scamming" stunts—such as kicking my opponent's ball out of the rough onto the fairway or kicking mine into the rough and behind a tree before I reached my drive.

I've played with guys who had a pal watching the match way out in the fairway, about where our tee shots would land. If I happened to hit a ball into the rough, 240 yards or so from the tee, the pal would kick my ball behind a tree or even pick it up and put it in his pocket. This meant a lost ball and a stroke penalty.

Or vice versa. If my opponent hit his ball into the rough or behind a tree, the pal would kick it out into the fairway to give the ball a good lie. Sometimes opponents would have their caddies instructed to get out in front and kick the balls around—kick mine back and kick theirs closer to the green.

These sharpies would also get to the caddies. If I asked my caddie on the putting green, "How do you think the ball will break—right or left?" the kid would be paid off to give the wrong reading. You could never make a six-foot putt. The kid would say, "It breaks sharply to the left," so you putt to the right of the hole and the ball breaks right, missing the hole by a mile.

The caddies would also "wrong club" you when they were paid off—advising you to use a seven iron when the distance from the green really called for a five iron, so that you'd end up short, even if you made a good shot.

I remember one day playing with some characters at Bayshore, a public course in Miami Beach. It was a close match, going into the eighteenth hole. A friend of mine was walking around the course with me, watching the action and the golf. My drive on the par-five eighteenth hooked into the woods. When I got to the ball, I found I had an almost impossible lie, behind a tree. My friend whispered, "I saw a guy kick your ball behind the tree." It made me furious—but determined to get out somehow. The only way I could hit my shot was to use an iron upside down. I swung as best I could and hacked the ball onto the fairway. I hit my third shot short of the green and into a sand trap. My opponents were grinning. That made me even madder. I took my sand wedge and blasted the ball two feet from the pin and made the putt—for a par five. I won the Nassau by a single stroke from two guys who were no longer smiling. But I had a grin a mile wide on my face. They knew that I knew they had kicked my ball. I never played with them again.

Some of the guys I bet with went around and changed the course on me. They liked to bet me that I couldn't break eighty. At the time I was just about an eighty shooter. But they'd say, "You've got to play from the back of the tees." They'd get up at the

1. This year, 1939, I won the Wimbledon triple crown.

2. *My first wife, Kay Fischer, at Forest Hills during the U. S. Professional Championships, 1946.*

3. *After being bitten by the golf bug, I got out of tennis altogether and hardly touched a racket for the next sixteen years.*

7. *I presented Margaret Court with a Mother's Day bouquet of red roses before our match . . .*

8. *. . . and I tried to console her afterward.*

9. "The Libber vs. The Lobber." *Billie Jean, Wimbledon winner, and I agree to meet in a $100,000 winner-take-all match.*

crack of dawn, go to the greenkeeper, and give him twenty dollars to put all the pins in the toughest places on the greens, as they do for the touring pros. It was pretty hard to take the bookies' money.

There was one fellow who liked to bet that I couldn't break forty on a given nine holes. He'd walk along with me when I was playing in a foursome, for our usual Nassau bets. He would bet me $500 that I could not break forty in the first nine. I'd score thirty-eight or thirty-nine. He wouldn't bet on the second nine—and I'd take a forty-one or more. The next round he'd lay off the first nine, and I'd be over forty. He'd come in with a bet on the second nine and I'd shoot thirty-eight. It was uncanny. He never guessed the right nine. I must have won ten bets from him in a row. He finally got tired of that game and left me alone.

Another bookmaker liked to go round with Marty Stanovich, the Fat Man, and bet with him. One time I was in a foursome playing against the Fat Man and the Fireman. Marty hooked his drive on the first hole, went out of bounds and ended up with a seven. He hooked again off the second tee and finished the hole with a six. The bookmaker then offered to bet Marty $5,000 that he couldn't break seventy on the round. Although he was already four over par on the first two holes, the Fat Man took the bet.

The Fat Man then proceeded to score eight successive threes—and the sequence included a par-five hole and three par fours—and finished his round with sixty-nine. He won the $5,000 and also killed us in our Nassau bets. It was the greatest exhibition I've ever seen. The Fat Man was always at his best when the big chips were down. I never considered Marty a crooked hustler. He was always fair with me, never lied about his low handicap. He was just a tremendous pressure player.

Playing with the Fat Man was good for my game, because I was always under pressure. I was playing a lot by this time at Plandome Golf Club, near my home on Long Island.

My best scores came when there was considerable money riding on the matches. One day at Plandome I went around the course with a member I'd often played with before. We had a hundred-dollar Nassau going on the round and I won the first eighteen. We played a second round, with presses on each nine—doubling the bet—and I won that too. My opponent was desperate to get even, so he insisted on a third round. By this time I was getting into a groove and the course was as familiar to me as my own back yard. I ended up scoring a sixty-six—my all-time personal record—on the last eighteen. But that was the only satisfaction I got. My opponent's check for $5,400 bounced, he dropped out of the club and I never got paid off.

The most successful match I ever played was in 1969 at the Concord Hotel in the Catskills on a course that is well-named—the Monster. I'd been having a series of matches with this individual and I always gave him a handicap. We had never seen the Monster before, and it turned out to be one of the longest and most difficult courses I've ever played.

We had ten different Nassaus going all at once. I was playing him even, giving him one shot, giving him two shots, and three, four, five, six, seven, eight and nine shots. And every match was played four ways

—the front nine, the back nine twice and the eighteen hole total. In addition, we had automatic presses on all the bets. This is what I call action.

When the smoke cleared that day, I had beaten my opponent fifty-two different ways. The stakes were $100 Nassau, so I ended up with $5,200 on the eighteen holes.

I had been playing tennis again for about a year by this time, so I offered my opponent a chance to get even by betting against me on the tennis court. A couple of my old tennis rivals were staying at the Concord at the same time. They offered to play me two against one for $500 a set. My golfing pal hopped in and bet me $1,000, hoping to recoup some of his losses. But I won three sets in a row and another $4,500 from the three guys. It was a pretty good day's work, and none of the checks bounced.

But I've got a drawer full of bad checks, running into thousands of dollars, from golfing deadbeats or guys who were in over their heads. A guy will want to act like a big shot but can't back it up—hand you a check and then stop payment. Or lose a match and leave town, and you'd never see him again. And you can't take a guy to court over a gambling debt.

By all odds the most action I ever got on the golf course was at the Greenbrier in White Sulphur Springs, playing an oil man from Indiana. This was a year or so after I had taken up golf.

I'd played this millionaire earlier that year in Florida, and we ended up about even in the betting. I had played in a Calcutta pool event at White Sulphur Springs, which was won by William Ford, of the Ford

Motor family, a strong golfer who could outhit most of the pros, and a pro partner. I had not done well in the Calcutta, so I stayed over at the hotel to practice. The oil man showed up and I got involved in a match with him. He had not been playing much, so he worked out a bet with me that would have been good for him if he'd been playing as well then as he had been in Florida earlier in the year.

I gave him a stroke on every hole but the par threes—that amounted to fourteen strokes for the round. We started out playing $1,000 Nassau. He started so badly on the front nine that he wanted to press when he got two holes down and make a fresh bet. He lost each press. When it was all over that first day, he had lost about $10,000.

The next day he wanted to raise the stakes. Since I was now playing on his money, I had nothing to lose and I said okay. But I had to give him a stroke on every hole, including the par threes, for a total of eighteen. It didn't make any difference, he played so badly. He blew up from his regular one-hundred game to about one thirty-five. I was still shooting my regular eighty-five. So he ended the second day $20,000 down to me. By the time the week was over, although I kept increasing his handicap, he had lost $180,000. He also lost another bundle to a baseball owner who was in our foursome.

But there is a sequel to the story. A few weeks later in New York, the oil man invited me to a suite in the Sherry Netherland Hotel, where he had organized a gin rummy game. My poor luck with cards was running as usual. So the oil man, an excellent gin player, took most of my golf winnings away from me in a couple of sessions at cards.

Dizzy Dean was as good a golfer as he was a baseball pitcher—or so it seemed to me. I could rarely beat him, although he was generous in giving me handicaps. But one day Dizzy bet me $100 Nassau with this handicap—that he would putt on every green with his wooden driver, allowing me to use my putter. Since putting is the strong point of my game, I was able to beat him that day, for a change.

Dizzy had the reputation of being one of the most successful golf bettors of them all. The story is that when Dizzy was the radio announcer for a major league team, he was beating the owner badly at golf, so the owner dropped his radio contract—Dizzy was costing the boss too much money on the links.

Dizzy's stature as a Baseball Hall of Famer meant a lot down in Texas with the big oil men.

"I'm playing you two-hundred Nassau and giving you two and two," he'd say at the beginning of a match. "And you over there, I'm giving you five shots for two hundred dollars."

Dizzy might have been able to give them more of a handicap, but the players would just say, "Yes, Diz; anything you say; fine, Diz." No arguments, no negotiating with the great Dizzy Dean. In his golf action, Dizzy won about 95 percent of his matches from millionaires who were afraid to talk back to him. He had a beautiful thing going for him and, so far as I know, still has.

George Morton Levy, former owner of Roosevelt

Raceway, was another high-stakes golfer. I once played in a foursome with Levy and Dizzy Dean. Dean bet Levy a $200 Nassau and gave him twelve shots—six on each nine. I said to Levy, "I'll play you, but I'll only give you three on each nine." Levy thought he should get more—mainly because of the phony reputation I had acquired through the *Life* publicity. Dizzy killed Levy in their bet, winning three or four ways, including presses.

I was having a bad day, shooting a ninety or ninety-one instead of my usual eighty-five. So it came down to the eighteenth hole between Levy and myself, and I eked out a win which cost Levy $200.

He had lost three or four times that much to Dizzy but Levy concentrated his annoyance on me, not the big guy. "What are you, some kind of hustler?" Levy asked as he paid off. He never said a word to Dean.

Levy and others judged me guilty by association of being a hustler because of the bad publicity. They did not read the small print in the *Life* article which said I was a square guy who could not shoot very well but was a tough competitor.

A lot of guys were actually afraid to play with me because of that phony reputation. Many times, especially when I was in over my head with the Fat Man or other really good golfers, I had occasion to wish that I could live up to my press notices. In other words, I had the name but not the game.

Jack Kramer is a tough man to win a bet from—in tennis or anything else. He likes to boast that he *never* loses a bet. But it's not true.

I won $200 from Jack on the golf course, not by beating him but by taking a match from his great pal, Ted Schroeder. Jack thought highly of Ted's golf game and put up the money with great confidence. Everybody was surprised when I beat Ted. But Jack brooded about it.

We went out to dinner in New York that night and Jack had a few cocktails. We got to reminiscing about a great match at Forest Hills in 1948, when Jack played Don Budge for the first time in his life. It was in the semifinals of the professional championships and I remembered the match well. I had already got through to the finals, so I was going to play the winner of this match. I wanted Budge to win, since I'd been beating him on the pro tour, and I watched every point closely. Kramer took the match in the fifth set, but I managed to beat him anyway in the finals.

As the drinks continued to flow, Jack insisted that he had not lost his service more than once in the fourth set of the semifinals, but I remembered clearly that he dropped serve twice. Jack wanted to bet my wife $10,000 that I was wrong, but I wouldn't let her take the bet. He wanted to bet me anything I wanted to name, but I didn't want to take his money. He finally became so insistent about it that I said, "Look, Jack, you've got two hundred dollars of mine which you owe me from the Schroeder match today. Want to give me ten-to-one odds? You've got my stake of two hundred dollars right there. If I win, I get twenty-two hundred dollars from you, is that right?"

He agreed, so we made the memory bet and Jack relaxed with another drink.

The next day I saw him at the marquee in Forest Hills, where a tournament was in progress. His eyes were bleary. I asked him where he had been.

"I went to the morgue at *The New York Times* and looked up the results of the 1948 pro matches," he answered. "You were right. I lost my service twice in the fourth set against Budge."

He took out his checkbook to pay me the $2,200. But I felt sorry for him,

I said, "Jack, you're in the promoting business and I'm retired. I've got a canvas court left over from my last tour. You can have it for three hundred dollars, although it's worth over a thousand. I'll also buy a five-hundred-dollar box for your Los Angeles matches."

I also agreed to give Schroeder a return match in LA. This time he beat me easily and Jack won back his $200.

After all, what with one thing and another I made very little profit out ot the $2,200 memory bet. It was one of the few bets you'll ever hear of Kramer losing, but he managed to get most of it back anyhow.

During my golfing years I made a lot of birdies and an eagle or two, but never an ace. However, the last match I ever played stands out in my memory.

I was in a foursome at the Greenacres Country Club in Trenton playing $100 Nassaus. About $1,000 was going to change hands. My partner had to go home after the first eighteen holes. So I continued the match alone, playing two balls against the other pair and taking the score of my better ball. In other words, I had myself for a partner. I liked to play this way. Some people would get tired playing two balls around a course, but I could do it all day long.

As we came in to the eighteenth green, there was quite a bit of money swinging on the match. It was a par-five hole and both my opponents were on the green in three. I hit a poor approach shot and landed short of the green in three. I took out the trusty sand wedge that Sam Snead gave me and pitched the ball into the hole for a birdie four. My opponents were so startled that both missed their birdie putts and I won the hole.

We wanted to play a third round but it was getting dark by then. So we retraced our steps to play only the final three holes—sixteenth, seventeenth and eighteenth.

At the eighteenth the same situation developed again. My opponents were on the green in three and I was short of the green. As I took out my sand wedge, I said, "Wouldn't it be funny if lightning struck again?"

"Oh, go on and shoot!" one of them yelled.

I swung the wedge, the ball landed in front of the hole and rolled into the cup for a birdie four. The two guys missed their birdie putts and I took all the money.

That was the last time I played golf. Open tennis had arrived on the scene by this time. I returned to the game at which I had been both amateur and professional world champion, to see if I could get back on top against the world's best middle-aged players.

5

PEOPLE ARE ALWAYS ASKING me which game, tennis or golf, I prefer and which I consider the better sport. My answer to both questions is tennis.

As one who has pretty good credentials in each of these sports, I think I'm qualified to discuss the differences between them better than most people. They are both lifetime sports. In these days of ever-increasing leisure time, more and more people are taking them up. What is the essential difference between the two popular pastimes?

The simplest answer is this: Tennis is an athletic contest, in which physical fitness is at a premium. Golf is a kind of outdoor billiards, with manual dexterity and proper mental approach at a premium.

In order to be a great tennis player you must, of necessity, be a great athlete. This is not to say it does not help a golfer to be athletic. There are many golfers. notably Gary Player of South Africa, who make an effort through daily exercise to stay in shape. Sam

114

Snead's long career as a tournament player is due partly to his fine physical condition. This was true of Ben Hogan in his day, as well.

On the other hand, golf is a mechanical game, a mental and psychological test. It's not a running and moving game. The ball is standing still; you are hitting a stationary object. You can take all the time you need to hit it. But this can be good or bad—you have time at each shot for the psychological pressure to build up. In professional golf $10,000 or more often hinges on a single putt of three feet. You see the top players walking around the ball, measuring the distance to the hole, trying to read the green, taking a deep breath. Sometimes a golfer is literally unable to move the club back to stroke the ball. In tennis it's possible to choke and hit a poor shot on a critical point, but I've never heard of a player who couldn't draw back his racket. In tennis you develop such physical momentum as the match goes on that stroking becomes an instinctive, mechanical business. It doesn't take on the psychological aspects to the same degree as in golf.

Having learned to play both games well, I would say that it is tougher to learn the complete repertoire of golf shots, the use of all the woods and irons in the right place at the right time, than it is to learn the various tennis strokes. I think proper instruction, at a young age, is imperative in order to produce a well-rounded golfer. Someone with an aptitude for tennis and an observant eye can learn to play well without formal instruction. However, before my friends in the tennis-teaching ranks jump on my back, let me hasten to add that good instruction will make you a better tennis player a lot quicker than the do-it-yourself method.

Ellsworth Vines is the only man I know who has been a tennis champion—he won the Forest Hills title twice and was professional champion—and also a successful golfer on the professional tour. He won a number of amateur and pro golf tournaments and was among the top fifteen money winners on the golf tour.

I asked Ellie which game he thought was tougher to play. He put it this way. He thought tennis was easier because the dimensions of the court are constant and the only difference between courts is their surface. The baselines and the lines are always the same distance from each other and the net is six inches higher at the ends than in the middle.

But in golf all courses are different, Ellie argued. Playing constantly on the golf tour, he had to cope with a number of courses, requiring a wide variety of shots. I disagree, for a lot of reasons.

No matter how much coordination and skill are required in golf, you can walk, stroll—and now *ride* in your golf cart—to the ball. You don't have to run down a ball against a man who is trying desperately to frustrate you by putting it out of your reach.

So I see tennis as the far more demanding game physically. Sam Snead, Julius Boros, Arnold Palmer and many other golfers in their forties, fifties and sixties are competing against, and beating, men half their age on the pro tour because of their greater experience and know-how. The difference in age doesn't make the difference in golf that it does in tennis. Only the rare

116

tennis player, such as Pancho Gonzales and Gardnar Mulloy, can survive on the tennis court against players half their age or less.

Golf requires great strength—witness Jack Nicklaus and his 385-yard drives—and great skill. But the great tennis player has the speed of a 100-yard sprinter and the stamina of a two-mile runner. Tennis players always have the *look* of an athlete. Many tournament golfers are overweight and anything but impressive specimens as they plod around the course in televised matches. I have never seen a tournament tennis player who was out of shape, except after a long layoff. The game forces you into condition and keeps you there.

At Wimbledon in 1970 I witnessed a tremendous battle between two physically strong, fit men—Roy Emerson and John Newcombe—which went to 11 to 9 in the fifth set. It was the hardest, fastest, most grueling tennis I'd watched in a long time, neither player letting up for a second in the three-hour marathon. They were like two heavyweight fighters going at it, hammer and tongs, for the full fifteen rounds. This was a classic example of the stamina required in big-time tennis.

Speed of foot is extremely important and agility even more so. The reason Gonzales remained a great player well into his forties was because he retained his agility. He was always as fluid in his movements as a boxer or fencer.

You also have to have a bit of the tactician in you to play top tennis. I think brains are important to a tennis player to that degree. You need not have been a scholar, but you have to use good judgment. You must be able to change tactics to turn a losing game into a winning game, and you must be able to keep the winning game from changing into a losing game. It's like being your own quarterback, calling the right plays on the field.

So in my book a tennis player is the complete athlete. He has to have the speed of a sprinter, the endurance of a marathon runner, the agility of a boxer or fencer and the gray matter of a good football quarterback. Baseball, football, basketball players are good athletes, but they don't need all these attributes to perform well.

I love baseball, but it's a comparatively slow game. A left fielder in a baseball game might catch three balls all afternoon, in the same amount of time that Emerson and Newcombe were hitting hundreds of shots—at top speed.

In addition to its sheer physical aspect, tennis has its mechanical demands as well. You must master the correct grips on forehand, backhand and service; you have to have the right body position in making your shots, use the right footwork and employ the correct follow-through. You must hit the ball as hard as you can and still control it. This is what Laver, Newcombe, Rosewall and Gonzales can do—hit the ball hard and still control it. When you start losing control, you are on a losing game. Ideal tennis is a game of *controlled speed.*

Little men have made some of the finest players— Frank Parker, Henri Cochet, Bitsy Grant, Ken Rosewall, Rod Laver and myself—because we could all control the ball as well as the taller players and were just as agile and quick about the court.

The will to win is perhaps even more important in tennis than it is in golf, although this intangible is hard to pin down. I think of Gonzales as the prime example of a man with the burning desire that produces victories. Gonzales at his best had a tremendous serve, true, but he never had the best mechanical game. He was not a penetrating volleyer, he didn't punch the ball with power the way Frank Sedgman or Tony Trabert did, or Ken Rosewall does off his backhand. Any number of players hit the ball harder than Gonzales did on the volley. He was a "catchy" volleyer, who would reach out and catch the volley, and he was good on the drop volley. But no one ever burned with a greater desire to win, and that is what has kept Gonzales in the top ranks of players for a quarter century.

Tennis is like boxing, in that it is a contest of one on one. Sugar Ray Robinson, one of the all-time greats in boxing, could control a match, make his opponent look bad. In tennis, the better player often controls his opponent in much the same way. But in golf you can't control your opponent. You are out there playing the golf course, playing against par. You are playing yourself, if you will.

For the average player of either golf or tennis, the exercise is a prime factor. Here tennis wins hands down. It is a physical workout, win or lose, and you are going to sweat a bit, no matter what the weather or temperature. It's just what the doctor ordered, for health reasons.

As for golf, the health aspect is practically nonexistent except for breathing fresh air. Golf was always a tremendous challenge to me, a great game, and I loved it. But one of the reasons I have gone back to tennis is the health factor. I have lost a lot of weight since taking up the racket again, feel better, sleep better. I can get a terrific workout in an hour or so.

This is a break for tennis wives too. A golfer usually has to spend an entire day to get in eighteen holes on a busy course. In tennis, a player can get the workout he needs and be back home again in a couple of hours.

One more thing about tennis versus golf: Form is more important in tennis. The better player almost always wins. This is not true in golf. There are low-handicap amateur golfers by the hundreds in this country who can beat the top professionals on the days they are shooting to their handicaps or better. Low-handicap golfers frequently shoot below their handicaps, since a handicap represents a golfer's *average* score, not his best-ever performance.

On the professional golf tour there are thirty or more tournaments in the year. It is rare for one player to win as many as five of these. But in tennis the top two or three players win most of the tournaments. One year as an amateur I won seventeen out of the eighteen tournaments I played during the summer season. That is a typical result when a tennis player becomes number one in the country.

In tennis it is not unusual for a certain player to beat another top-ranking player literally dozens of times without losing to him. I played Joe Hunt in official tournaments more than forty times and lost to him only three or four times. The same thing held true for Billy Talbert and Gardnar Mulloy. I was able to

120

beat Billy in all but one of forty matches. I never lost to Mulloy. In golf it is inconceivable that the U.S. Open Champion or the top money-winning golfer could beat any of the top thirty or forty touring golf pros forty consecutive times—or more than four or five —in head-to-head competition.

In golf there is nothing that a Palmer, Nicklaus, Trevino, Casper or any other top player can do about it if some lesser player gets hot and shoots a sixty-six while they are turning in a respectable sixty-eight or sixty-nine. But in tennis there is a great deal that a top player can do to control an opponent who happens to come into a hot streak.

You must learn to pace yourself in tennis. You see this all the time in tournament tennis—the old pro overcoming a kid who is burning up his reserves of nervous energy. Nervous exhaustion is a big factor in many matches. You use up energy very fast when you are keyed up for a big match. I've been through this many times myself and suffered from it, until experience taught me how to control myself and prevent nervousness from depleting my supply of energy.

In golf, I can't imagine anyone suffering from nervous exhaustion at the end of eighteen holes. You can get the jitters if there is a lot of money riding on the putts on the last green. But golf simply doesn't make the same physical demands on a player, or take the same physical toll, that tennis does, particularly on the tournament level.

To sum up, I have found tennis and golf to be quite different. But each has its own fascination, its own characteristics, its own demands and its own rewards.

6

ALL THROUGH THE YEARS that I was playing golf, first in Florida and then in the New York area, where my business was located, the thought of returning to tennis was in the back of my mind. I was having fun with golf but I knew that, despite an occasional subpar round, I'd never be an aging Jack Nicklaus. Tennis was my game. I had been the world champion. I still had the old desire to win. The senior-tournament circuit for players forty-five and over was beginning to perk up and a lot of my old rivals were playing in it.

When my forty-fifth birthday rolled around, I was panting to get back into competition. But there was a big barrier—I was still classified as a professional, and the senior tournaments were conducted on a strictly amateur basis by the USLTA, my old nemesis.

I went to see Gladys Heldman, publisher of *World Tennis* magazine and highly influential in the world of tennis. I tried to get Gladys to run an editorial urging the USLTA to drop its ban on pros competing in senior tournaments. She wasn't particularly interested in the idea, and nothing came of it.

But rumors were always springing up about open tennis coming in, so I decided to play tennis again in hopes they might materialize. I built a tennis court on our property in Plandome, Long Island, and invited the good young players of the area to work out with me. I also bought into a group of public courts in Woodside, Queens, where we put up plastic bubbles, air-supported temporary structures that were lighted and heated in the winter for indoor play. I did a lot of playing here as well.

But my favorite courts were on the roof of a thirteen-story commercial building in mid-Manhattan. They lay in the shadow of those tall red-white-and-blue-striped smokestacks anchored to a Con Edison power plant on the East River. This is no scenic spot—particularly when smoke is billowing around you in a river breeze. The balls get so dirty—absolutely black—from the soot settling on the courts that you are lucky to get one set out of them.

But the Tennis Center had other attractions for me. It is a private club, directed by a lively seventy-four-year-old businessman, Larry Fertig, who, like all the members, loves to put his money where his mouth is. This argumentative gang of brokers, professional men and businessmen are mostly middle-aged and fair-to-middling tennis players. But their passion for action more than compensates for lack of tennis talent. To a man, they are born bettors who wouldn't think of taking to the court without backing themselves with a modicum of cash. Sometimes the modicum stretches into a bet of $500 a set, when a player gets what he considers to be an attractive handicap. These players can afford that kind of wagering.

Another mark of distinction about the flock of birds on this rooftop is that they are extremely tough negotiators. They have devised a weird and wonderful system of handicapping me. This has nothing to do with the VASSS points system devised by Newport's Jimmy Van Alen. As for the ancient bisque handicapping, most of these guys think that's some kind of Italian ice cream.

They have imposed an ingenious variety of penalties on me over the years, which pretty well reduced the advantage I held over them as a lifelong tournament player.

On various occasions—and with substantial bets going—they have required me to play matches while handicapped in any one of these ways:

• Carrying an open umbrella in my left hand, even while serving.

• Carrying a weighted suitcase in my left hand, also while serving.

• Wearing an oversized overcoat, buttoned from neck to ankle. and heavy rubber galoshes.

• Burdened by weights around my waist, wrists and ankles.

• Tied with rope to my doubles partner, chain-gang style, to cut down our court coverage.

• Holding a leash with a dog—or two dogs—at the other end.

Those are only samples of the inventiveness of the

rooftop gang when it comes to bringing me down to their level of play and extracting money from me.

Hank Greenberg, the big, burly former baseball slugger and member of the Baseball Hall of Fame, is a rooftop regular and just about as tough a negotiator as I've ever met. Like myself, Hank loves to win and hates to lose.

The first time I played Hank on the sooty rooftop he demanded, "Give me the alleys." That meant I had to keep my shots inside the singles lines on the sides of the court, whereas he could use the extra width of the doubles alleys on each side. We were betting $500 a set, and I took the first set without too much trouble.

Hank then suggested that I forget about the alleys and give him a 40–love advantage in each game. That meant he had game point against me during the first three points of each game. I beat him this way too. Then he came up with a new idea.

"When I'm serving," Hank explained, "I can put the ball into either the right or left box, but you'll have to serve conventionally into first one and then the other." He stood in the middle of the baseline and would try to put his serve into either box out of my reach. I moved into the center of the court. By dint of wild lunging from one side to the other, I managed to squeak through the set and show a $1,500 profit for the day.

But as I mentioned, Hank hates to lose. So the next time I showed up on the rooftop, he was ready with another proposition, also new to me at the time.

"I'm going to put two chairs in the court on your

side of the net," Hank announced. "You'll have to run around them, and if I hit either chair with the ball, you lose the point. I can put the chairs anywhere except inside the service box."

That meant that I not only had to avoid the chairs in running for the ball but had to defend the chairs from his serves and drives as well. It was a screwy idea, but it appealed to me. I took Hank on for the usual $500 and, by leaping around like a frightened kangaroo, managed to win the set.

Obviously Hank had feared that I might win with the chairs. He had another proposition ready—substituting two park benches for the two chairs. He dragged out two benches, each four feet long with high backrests, and set them up right behind the service line on each side of the court, leaving only a narrow alley in the center between them.

Again I had to defend the big benches from Hank's ball and cover the whole court as well. He would drop-shot into the forecourt, then lob into the backcourt, so that I was forced to thread my way through the narrow space between the benches or around them or leap over them—all of which I did. But the handicap was too much for me. Hank got his five hundred bucks back on that set. I didn't have the stamina for a third set after all that bounding around the benches.

But after lunch I revived. Hank said, "Why do we always have to play your game, regular tennis? Why not a game that I think I can play better than you, paddle ball?" I had played paddle tennis and won several national titles, since it is just a miniature ver-

126

sion of regulation tennis. But paddle ball is played on an indoor handball court, using four walls as in squash, and is something else entirely, I discovered.

We went to an indoor club nearby, and after a few warm-up games I agreed to play Hank for $500 a game. But this time I was getting the handicap for a change—Hank gave me fifteen points out of twenty-one. It seemed like a generous handicap, but he beat me. I couldn't fathom the technique of handling the bounces. I agreed to play another game at fifteen out of twenty-one, provided I could have two bounces before hitting the ball instead of one. This enabled me to handle the ball bouncing off the walls, and I won my money back.

Hank calls me another Ty Cobb, not because of my baseball prowess but because I have such a compulsion to win at whatever I'm playing. Cobb was the kind of card player, for instance, who would stay at the table all night during a losing streak, until the cards started to come his way. He used to tire everybody out. I guess I'm pretty much the same way—but not at cards. I'm sure to lose at gin or poker to the guys who lose to me on the court.

At any rate, instead of playing another set in paddle ball, I challenged Hank to a foul-shooting contest on the basketball court at the indoor club. I played basketball in high school and am a better-than-average foul shooter. Hank knew this and refused to shoot against me. He offered to bet me $500 that I couldn't make twenty-two out of twenty-five throws from the foul line. I hadn't had a basketball in my hands for years, so I suggested fifteen out of twenty-five. But Hank was adamant and I finally took the bet on his terms.

I stood at the foul line and Hank stood beside me, taking the ball as it rebounded and handing it to me for the next shot. I was shooting pretty well, considering my long layoff from the game, and I could see Hank getting worried as I swished the ball through the net. I reached the crucial point of twenty-one baskets out of twenty-four throws. The next shot could win the bet for me. But instead of tossing me the ball, Hank said disgustedly. "I've blown the bet," and hurled the ball across the court. I had to go and retrieve it and settle myself again at the foul line. I missed the shot. Hank had upset my rhythm in a beautiful example of gamesmanship. Like I said—he hates to lose.

Another regular at the Tennis Center at one time was Jack Dreyfus, who has one of the keenest betting minds of anyone. Before he founded the Dreyfus Fund, which he ran up to over a billion dollars in assets, Jack used to go to the trotters every night. He was such a fine handicapper that he made plenty of money this way, in his spare time. He is also a first-rate bridge and gin-rummy player, able to hold his own against the best in the world. Jack is also a golfer with a low handicap, who won his club championship ten years in a row. He did not take up tennis until he was in his late forties. As a result he has an un-orthodox style, using a forehand chop instead of a drive, and turning his racket over on the backhand side, so that he hits both forehands and backhands with the same side of the racket. But he is extremely fit physically, runs well and is a tremendous competitor.

It's almost impossible to win a dollar from Dreyfus. He knows every angle and can sense what's going to happen on the court. At the beginning I gave him 40–love and the alleys and won a set or two from him, at $1,000 a set. But he quickly improved to the point where I had to take the alleys away from him and reduce the points handicap to 30–love or less. He was winning about half the time that way.

Then he suggested a handicap of his own.

"Covering the whole court is too tough for me," he said. "What I want to do is divide the court in two on my side, by extending the center service line all the way from the baseline to the net, and play only one half."

That meant Jack could hit into my entire court but I was restricted to half of his. I couldn't keep the ball away from him and he was able to defend handily. I had to call off that game; it was costing me money.

Jack loves to play with guys better than he is— for the right handicap. The year Ken Rosewall won the French championships, he stayed at my home on Long Island for a couple of weeks. I arranged for Ken to partner Jack, against Tony Vincent, a very good senior player in New York, and me. In view of Ken's great ability, we played without a handicap for $500 a set. Jack was doing all the betting for his side, since Ken has never bet on himself. We played seven sessions in all, and Tony and I proved too strong for our opponents. Jack Dreyfus not only paid us off but also handed Ken a check for $1,500 for his services as partner. That came as no surprise to me. I knew about Jack's many generosities. He likes to give new Rolls

Royces to his pals. He gave one as a Christmas present to his tennis teacher, Solly Goldman.

But Jack hates to lose as much as I do. So he suggested then that I play singles with Rosewall, with him backing Ken at $500 a set. I agreed to the bet, if Ken would give me the alleys. I should have known better. Ken beat me easily, showing me the big difference betwen thirty-five and fifty, our respective ages at the time. We played another set, with Ken giving me the alleys, plus two games. The result was the same, although a bit closer. So I suggested one more set. Ken gave me the alleys, two games and 15–love in points. I finally managed to beat him that way. By that time Jack had to leave for the races—he owns the successful Hobeau Farms stable—and he went away satisfied, having recouped most of his losses from me.

I play a lot of doubles against Jack with a variety of partners, and at the end of a year we end up pretty even in our betting. We do all kinds of handicapping, and the negotiating beforehand is often more heated than our arguments on the court. But it all adds to the fun. Nobody gets hurt financially (who's going to hurt Jack?), and if I win money on the court, I'm sure to go inside and lose it at gin or backgammon.

Another well-known businessman who took up tennis late in life is Kirk Kerkorian, of Las Vegas and Hollywood. He was a fine athlete as a young man, a boxer, and this has helped him in taking up tennis. He loves the challenge and the movement of the game and is improving constantly. Having lived in Las Vegas for years, he understands gambling and is a real action guy. Like Dreyfus, he is a tough negotiator. He'd rather *give* me $1,000 than *lose* $100 in competition. One reason these men get to the top in the business world is that they drive a hard bargain—and this carries over to the games they play.

Alan King, the comedian, was a fine golfer who once haunted the fairways, as a player and also a spectator at the U.S. Open, the Masters and other big events, where he was a favorite with the pros. Now Alan has given up golf completely and become a tennis buff of the first order. He arranges his theatrical appearances on the road to coincide with the travels of the touring pros. He is always at home on Long Island for the U.S. Open at Forest Hills in September. Alan stages celebrity tournaments. with such enthusiastic players as song writer Burt Bacharach and film stars Charlton Heston, Dinah Shore and Dina Merrill, playing with John Newcombe, Rod Laver, Pancho Gonzales and other pros.

Alan and four other guys once challenged me for $100 a set. I played singles against the fivesome, but the traffic jam on their side of the net was so heavy that I beat the mob easily.

Alan has been improving recently, so much so that he has asked John Newcombe to be his partner against Pancho Segura and myself—for the right handicap. If we can ever work out a handicap that suits both Alan and me, we'll play the match.

Alan is an ingenious guy when it comes to betting. But he hasn't discovered the favorite stunt of Gil Hall, a top senior player a few years ago. Gil would offer to play the best player of his time—Bill Tilden, for example—without a racket. Gil used his bare hands for catching and throwing the ball back. It's really a trap, but you have to try it to believe it. The tennis player, using a racket, can't even win a game from his opponent, who can catch even Gonzales's bullet serves and throw the ball across the net out of reach.

Another tough handicap is for me and my partner to play doubles with just one racket between us, against a pair properly equipped with two rackets. Two ordinary players could beat Rod Laver and me this way, with Rod and me having to take alternate shots and pass the racket back and forth between us. I've lost money trying this one. The inventor of this game is another regular, Bernie Needle.

Another keen competitor is Len Hartman, a good senior player who operates several tennis courts in the metropolitan New York area. He likes a friendly bet of $100 a set, with a suitable handicap. He has worked out a system of weight handicaps to slow me down. I have to put on a belt that weighs twelve pounds, ankle weights of three pounds each and wrist weights of a pound and a half each. When I'm laden down like that, Len can play me even. This shows the mistake players make by going out on a court fifteen or twenty pounds overweight. The excess weight can make the difference between winning and losing. By the way, I have discovered that playing with weights is a good reducing gimmick in itself.

Most of the mob at the Tennis Center are too set in their ways, as I am, to take up VASSS—Jimmy Van Alen's Simplified Scoring System. This is a simple point-scoring system, similar to table tennis scoring, with twenty-one or thirty-one points comprising a match. Despite the advantages of VASSS, particularly for handicapping and betting, we have found it difficult to switch over from the traditional tennis scoring we have used all our lives. The rhythm of VASSS is all wrong for players used to deuce-ad scoring. There is such a thing as "playing to the score," which can be of vital importance in a match. It doesn't exist in VASSS.

However, there is one feature of VASSS which has been widely adopted and has some merit, in my opinion. That is the sudden-death tie breaker, which is in effect at the U.S. Open Championships at Forest Hills and which is being used, with some modification, by the World Championship Tennis group and at Wimbledon. At Forest Hills the exciting nine-point version is played when sets reach 6 all. The first player to win five points takes the set. If the two players are tied 4–4 in points, the next point becomes the sudden-death point, determining the winner of the set, which is then scored 7 to 6. In the modification used by the WCT players, a twelve-point tie breaker is used. But if players are tied at six points apiece, there is no sudden-death point, since the tie-breaker sequence must be won by a margin of at least two points. Theoretically, a twelve-point tie breaker could go on indefinitely, but in practice it's usually over quickly, and the set is also scored 7 to 6.

The tie breaker is a boon to tournament directors, since it prevents marathon matches, which sometimes run over to the following day and raise hell with the schedule. It also places TV coverage on a stricter time schedule, since matches will run to a specified length.

However, a tie breaker helps the lesser player more than it does the champions, who possess great stamina as well as fine strokes. Therefore I would like to see the tie breaker used at all times except in the really big, important tournaments. I like the way Wimbledon does it. There a tie breaker is used in every set except the fifth set of a long match. In this way the factors of stamina, endurance and physical fitness retain their importance, without stretching a match out to the ridiculous extremes of eighty, ninety or more games, with everybody, particularly the players, dying to see the end.

Another change, which in my opinion is long overdue and much needed, is reducing the importance of the serve. I am pretty much a traditionalist, but no game is so perfect it cannot be improved. As it is now, particularly on fast surfaces, such as grass, cement and indoors on wood, just one shot—a big first serve—can dominate the game completely. This nullifies the other shots in a great game—the overhead, the forehand, the backhand, the short angle shot, the touch shot.

Something must be done to take the enormous advantage away from the big server. Maybe allowing just one serve would do the trick. Maybe a rule should be introduced requiring the ball to bounce once on the server's side of the net before he can go in to volley. Either one of these changes—or perhaps both—might be the answer. Nothing is so monotonous for a gallery—or a large TV audience—as the bang-bang pace of the big serve-and-volley game. Points are decided with just three shots—serve, return and put-away volley. Rallies are rare. There is no chance for tactical and strategic moves. It is mindless tennis. It should be brought under control. Synthetic court surfaces can be made slow enough to cut down the server's advantage and discourage net rushing. I believe that a universal surface will be developed one day, for both indoor and outdoor play, which will encourage good ground strokes and long rallies and help to give the customers their money's worth.

7

In 1968 came the revolution: Open tennis was suddenly a reality. Amazingly enough it was the English tennis association which announced that Wimbledon, the Holy of Holies of amateur tennis, henceforth would be open to all players—amateurs, shamateurs, professionals —who could qualify on their merits. The knowledgeable people who run Wimbledon had finally gotten sick and tired of the hypocrisy of amateur tennis. Besides, they needed Rod Laver, Roy Emerson, Arthur Ashe, Ken Rosewall and other top professionals if they were to live up to their boast of putting on the world's greatest tournament.

I was fifty-one years of age when I finally became eligible for senior tournaments. I was bored with business and had a lot of leisure time on my hands. I welcomed the chance, late as it was, to get back into competition with players of my age and ability—and with those six years younger in senior ranks. Such fine players as Gar Mulloy, Vic Seixas, Tom Brown and Jaroslav Drobny were coming back to the game.

10. *When the odds are right and the money interesting I'll play with special handicaps.*

The first thing I did was work off the rubber tire I had accumulated around my middle during the years of playing golf and social tennis. I undertook a rigid schedule of dieting and exercise to regain the fitness which is vital to tournament tennis—even the comparatively slow-motion variety in senior tennis.

I got into a sweat suit every morning and ran around my home golf course, miles at a time, up and down hills, past my old buddies in their golf carts, who thought I had suddenly gone nuts. But the hard work paid off.

I dropped about twenty pounds, got back the spring in my fifty-one-year-old legs, practiced tennis every day and regained a semblance of my old stamina. I felt that I was probably as fit as anyone in my age group.

Letting me back into tennis was like giving me a new toy. I was amazed to find out that I could play twenty or thirty tournaments a year in such lush places as Acapulco, the Grand Bahamas, La Costa, Puerto Rico and Las Vegas—as well as Wimbledon and Forest Hills, where I had won the amateur titles in 1939. There were even international team competitions, modeled on the Davis Cup, with Swedish stars Lennart Bergelin and Torsten Johansson, Australia's Bob Howe and Frank Sedgman, and Gustavo Palafox of Mexico. I shook my head and swore at the stupid amateur rules that had kept me out of this lovely senior circuit for so many years.

Now I was ready to return to Wimbledon, something I had dreamed of doing ever since I won my triple Wimbledon championship—men's singles, men's doubles and mixed doubles—twenty-nine years earlier.

Wimbledon holds a senior doubles event—but no senior singles—along with the regular tournament each year. My old buddy from amateur and pro ranks, Pancho Segura, was still active in California and playing his steady, heady game. I was sure we could win the doubles at Wimbledon, and I went around making all the bets I could in London before the big show, the first open-tennis tournament, began at Wimbledon, in June of 1968.

Wimbledon is the world's number-one tennis event and perhaps always will be. It is without question the world's most efficiently run tournament, apart from its glamour. It gives a player an enormous lift just to be part of the scene. The huge, knowledgeable crowds are milling all around. The electricity comes at you in waves. If ever a player rises to the occasion, it is at Wimbledon. Even royalty attends, and players on the Centre Court stop play and bow politely when members of the Royal Family enter the royal box.

The Centre Court, or Enclosure, enables the crowd to surround you, rather than sit high above you as at Forest Hills. You can *feel* the spectators all around you. And the British are good sports. They appreciate good tennis. The applause always comes in the right places. They know tennis and they know the players, and the players respond by giving their best performances. This makes Wimbledon the most exciting tennis occasion of the year.

The grass courts there are better than any others I've ever played on. They are faster than those at Forest Hills. The grass may turn brown in spots during the course of the two weeks of constant play, but you get very few bad bounces and the courts remain firm right up to the final weekend.

They cut the grass so close and roll it so hard that the ball bounces higher than on most grass courts and you can make better shots. In case of rain they have large tarpaulins to cover the principal courts. They don't become saturated as they do at Forest Hills, where the tournament is often delayed for days at a time by heavy rains.

The entire atmosphere of Wimbledon is unique. The newspapers give it enormous coverage and the matches are on BBC television all day long—without affecting the attendance one bit. Wimbledon is *the* place to be for tennis fans. It's been like that for more than seventy years. It's a fixture of the English sports scene. People queue up for tickets, even standing outside the windows all night long, since Wimbledon is sold out long before it opens each year. A Centre Court seat is a valued property and is handed down in wills from father to son.

The players are pampered at Wimbledon as nowhere else in the world. Chauffeured limousines pick them up at their London hotels and take them back in the evening. The players have their own lounge, where they can watch matches in progress while they eat or relax. The scoreboards are so situated that you can follow the progress of play on a dozen courts at the same time from the players' lounge. The organization of the whole event is something special.

The fact that the bookmakers publish a line of betting odds on tennis strikes me as a particularly civilized thing to do. But I got a rude shock when I went back to Wimbledon and tried to get a bet down on Segura and me. I had made a great clean-up betting on myself to turn the hat trick in 1939. But this time the bookmakers turned me down. They accept bets now only on men's and women's singles, not on senior events. So I was confined to making friendly bets with other players or the people I knew among the spectators.

A few hours before the start of the senior doubles disaster struck and I had to call off all bets.

Pancho and I had put in a good day's practice. We were both in great shape and felt confident that we could lick the field, even though it included such familiar names as Jaroslav Drobny, Bill Talbert and other former champions.

I went to bed early. The night was unusually hot and sultry for London, so I opened a large door in our hotel suite that opened onto a balcony. Sometime during the night I became conscious of a draft. I got up and went to close the door, a heavy steel-and-glass affair which went from floor to ceiling. I took the curtains in one hand and pulled the door shut with the other. Unfortunately the thumb of my right hand, holding the curtains, was caught in the crack, and the huge door closed on it, nearly severing the finger.

The thumb was operated on that night and put in a cast. That was the end of my Wimbledon dream and nearly the end of the finger. It was touch-and-go for a while whether I might lose it, but, despite postoperative infection, it healed completely and is now as good as ever.

So my Wimbledon debut as a pro had to be postponed. I went back finally in 1970, after I had been playing and doing well on the growing senior international circuit for two years, and won the senior doubles title with Drobny. Wimbledon was everything I had recalled, and my only disappointment was not being able to get a bet down with my old bookmaker.

Although the grass at Wimbledon is superb, it's the only place that can make that claim. I am in favor of replacing grass—even at Wimbledon—with some kind of synthetic surface. This is particularly necessary in international competition, notably the Davis Cup for men, the Federation Cup for women and the Stevens Cup in senior tennis. Only four countries— England, Australia, Canada and the United States— have any grass courts, and the vast majority of the players even in those countries have never set foot on one. Why continue to use a surface which unfairly penalizes the overwhelming number of tournament players, now that synthetic courts are available in a wide variety of types and makes?

Although the game was first played on an English lawn, grass is hopelessly dated from a practical standpoint. It costs the West Side Tennis Club at Forest Hills more than $50,000 a year to maintain its fifty-odd grass courts. They are out of action six months of the year and can only be played on four days a week in season! That is really luxury living.

Because of a number of factors, including the weather and a difference in the types of grass that can be grown, the surface at Forest Hills is far inferior to Wimbledon. It is soft and bumpy and cuts up easily at tournament time each September, and players beef constantly about bad bounces. Rod Laver once cried, "This stuff is no good for anything but feeding sheep!"

Due to players' complaints, the West Side Tennis Club decided to replace about fifteen of the grass courts at Forest Hills with a composition surface which is somewhat faster than clay and is quick-drying. Such a changeover should meet with the approval not only of the players but the spectators. They are inconvenienced almost every year by interruptions and postponements of play due to wet grass, which takes far longer to dry than any of the newer surfaces. As a native-born Californian, I grew up on cement courts, which are as fast as grass, and I play well on that smooth, even surface. However I agree with Jack Kramer, Billy Talbert and other tournament directors that the public is far better served by the slower synthetic or composition courts. Now that television has become a vital factor in tennis, and matches have been shortened by means of tie-breaker scoring to fit into TV time slots, the game should be further enlivened for the viewing audience by giving them the long rallies and more entertaining kind of tennis provided by a slow surface.

One reason that women's tennis is suddenly becoming popular is not only the advent of such great young players as Chris Evert of Florida and Evonne Goolagong of Australia—the public also is fascinated by exciting contests featuring long rallies, with the ball crossing the net a dozen times or more on each point. This is standard fare in the women's game. It is also the rule in men's senior tennis, which I contend should be getting the same recognition—and prize money—as women's tennis.

I'm having more fun playing senior tennis than I ever had as a junior champion or on the amateur and pro circuits. I don't believe there is anyone who plays more regularly. That's an important part of the reason why I have been able to capture so many senior championships—that, plus the old desire to win, which has never left me. Even though I'm up against players seven years younger, I usually win because the match seems to mean more to me. And I usually have $50 or $100 riding on myself to bring out my best playing.

My game was made to order for senior tennis, with its long rallies, lobbing tactics, retrieving and emphasis on backcourt play. *Sports Illustrated* magazine described my game as "Chips, chops, drops and lobs." The magazine went on to say that "a game between two deftly confident senior players can achieve high excitement and produce the kind of shotmaking a great many weekend players might do well to emulate." One reason for the growing galleries at our senior tournaments is that a lot of older players realize they can learn more about playing tennis from watching us than they can by watching a pair of net-charging kids whale the devil out of service-and-volley in a type of play beyond the capabilities of mature men. There are at least twenty senior tournaments in Europe and the United States, in addition to Wimbledon, which attract an extremely fine class of player. They are held in such places as Acapulco, Puerto Rico, the Grand Bahamas, Las Vegas, La Jolla and the La Costa Club in California, and in Monte Carlo, which is not exactly a slum circuit. The atmosphere of these events is like that of a college class reunion. We get together to reminisce and lie a little bit about the old days—but still beat each other with as much enthusiasm as ever.

The Stevens Cup, modeled on the Davis Cup format, is by all odds the finest American senior competition. Teams from eleven nations entered the Stevens Cup in 1971, and the number is increasing every year. Each tie (team match) consists of four singles and one doubles match, as in Davis Cup play. I played both singles and doubles in the 1971 challenge round, held at the Town Tennis Club in New York City, where the U.S. team of Tony Vincent, Gus Palafox (formerly of Mexico) and I defeated an Australian team, Bob Howe and Jim Gilchrist, three matches to two. The Aussies led us 2 to 1 after winning the doubles on the second day. The third day produced a close finish, with Palafox beating Howe to even the tie at 2 all. I won over Gilchrist in the deciding match. It was an exciting day, a typical one in these international matches. Many people told us they enjoyed our challenge round as much as any they had ever watched in Davis Cup competition.

One thing you can say about senior tennis—the galleries get their fill of watching the balls go by. In my Stevens Cup match with Gilchrist, a linesman took count of one rally—the ball crossed the net exactly 147 times, with both of us hugging the baseline, never venturing to the net. A few days earlier Gilchrist and I were playing a practice set at Forest Hills. One club member who was idly watching us went to the bar for a drink. When he came back about twenty minutes later, Jim and I were still playing the same point. That's senior tennis!

What we lack in speed in senior ranks we make up for in grim determination. I've worked harder on the court in senior play than I ever did in my life before. One reason may be that the rallies are so long. We don't use tie breakers, and sets can run on forever.

During the Dubler International Cup matches in La Jolla, between U.S. seniors and the Swedish team that had beaten everybody in Europe, I lost a tough singles match to Lennar Bergelin. Afterward I played another guy two practice sets. I felt that was enough singles play, since I was up for another Dubler Cup singles match, with Torsten Johansson, the following day.

But a young English player came up and suggested we play one set, for a side bet of $200. He offered me a two-game handicap, and I took him on. He won the set, so I asked him to play me another with the same handicap. I won the second set. He asked for a third set, which I also won. By this time I had begun to feel a bit weary. But since I was holding all the money, I had to agree to play him a final set.

The score went to 6 to 7, with me leading at 30 all. The captain of the U.S. senior team, Emory Neale, who had been anxiously watching the match, came up to the fence.

"Gee, Bobby, you're playing too much," he said. "You'll be dead tomorrow and we need you for that match with Johansson."

I yelled back, "Okay, I've got him now." It was match point.

With that the English youngster hit a wide ball. I

raced to put it away and took a nasty spill. Both elbows and knees were scraped and bleeding, and my right ear was also torn and oozing drops of blood. Someone rushed over and picked me up. My shirt and shorts were bloody. I looked like a Vietnam casualty.

Neale was furious. He rushed over and yelled, "Please call this match off!"

My opponent, who was a couple of hundred bucks in the hole, agreed. "Okay, let's call it off with everything even."

I wasn't about to quit while I was ahead in the betting.

"Let's finish the set," I replied, somehow stanching the flow from my elbows, knees and ear.

We resumed playing, and the points and games went on—and on and on and on. We finally finished under the lights about midnight. I won the set 16 to 14 and collected my winnings.

My opponent, knowing I was as dead tired as he was, promptly bet me that I would lose to Johansson next day. But a good night's sleep did me a lot of good. Johansson had beaten me twice that year, so I was able to get odds of 2 to 1, with me on the short end, in a number of bets that I made on the scene and by telephone around the country. Wounds and all, I beat Johansson in straight sets for a nice payday. That win also gave our team the winning margin over the Swedes.

A lot of people may still insist that tennis is a sissy sport. But they haven't played senior tennis. I once played fourteen sets of senior singles in one day on a cement court in California. As a result, my right leg broke down and I developed a severe case of shin splints. But I was due to play in a big senior tournament starting the next week in Haiti, so I bandaged the leg and flew down to Port au Prince. Despite the leg injury, I reached the finals against Al Doyle. I asked my doubles partner, Len Hartman, if he wanted to bet on Doyle, one of the finest senior players in the country. Knowing how bad my leg was, Hartman bet me Doyle would win. Then I went into the stands before the match, trying to get other bets down. But I had no luck. Tony Vincent said, "If I bet you, you'll take the bandages off and start playing." Obviously Tony didn't think my leg was as bad as it looked.

I lost the first set to Doyle but was still full of confidence that I could beat him on one leg. I ran back into the stands and tried to get someone to back Doyle, now a set up on me. Nobody was willing to bet on him, even with that edge. That turned out to be a break for me. Doyle took the second set and the match. The only one I had to pay off was Hartman.

A somewhat similar experience happened during the Pacific Southwest senior tournament at Newport Beach. I was due to play Sammy Match in the singles final. I went into the crowd and spoke to a lot of high rollers but couldn't get any action. I even offered to give odds on myself but got no takers. Match beat me 6–3, 6–3. The high rollers were eating their hearts out, so I had no trouble getting $4,500 on Match and me in the doubles final that followed. We were to play Dick Mateer and Ed Carter, who are both over six feet tall and have two of the best serves in senior tennis. Match is about my height.

Sammy and I lost the first set. I called my brother John down to the side of the court. I told him to ask the high rollers if they wanted to double their bets, now that we were a set down.

"They ought to give me two-to-one odds, but I'll take even money," I told John.

The guys all doubled their bets—at even money. Sammy and I won the second set to square the match. But Mateer and Carter were outserving us in the final set. They got a service break and led 4 to 3 with Mateer's service to come. Somehow we broke him back and then broke Carter for the match. I collected $9,000 for the day. which was not bad at all, considering I had lost my singles match, which would have cost me plenty if I'd been able to bet on it.

The stimulus provided by the big bet helped to win that one for us. I recall another instance where a bet made the difference. At Knoxville, where I was playing in the annual senior tournament, I agreed to play the club pro, Bill Silvia, on the morning of the finals. Bill would only bet me five dollars a set and he beat me 6–2, 6–1. I then went out and won the senior singles and doubles finals. Some club members got together and collected $1,000 to back Silvia against me in a return match. I agreed to play, even though I had just come off the court after two finals. This time I beat the pro 6–4, 7–5. Of course, I was accused of hustling the club members into the big bet by deliberately losing to Silvia in the morning. But what made the difference between the two matches for me was the difference between $10 and $1,000. I was exactly $990 better the second time.

8

THE FACT that tennis originated on the lawns of upper-class England and was imported early to Newport and other social centers in this country contributed to its reputation as a snob or sissy sport. However, even more harmful to the sport's reputation is the widespread suspicion that the game attracts homosexuals of both sexes more than other sports do.

As far as men's tennis goes, I know from forty-four years of exposure to hundreds and hundreds of players that the suspicion has no foundation in fact.

I know of just two men players who have been tagged as practicing homosexuals—Bill Tilden and Baron Gottfried von Cram. Both went to jail for these activities—Tilden in California and von Cram in Germany. Some people thought von Cram was framed and that Hitler put him in jail because he was anti-Nazi and not because of his sexual preferences. That may or may not be true. I know that von Cram had a reputation for being queer among the players of his day, although he was married for a time to Barbara Hutton.

I had no personal knowledge of von Cram's sex tendencies.

With Tilden it was a different matter. He never made passes at fellow players, so far as I know, but he was overly fond of ball boys. He was also a born prima donna, an actor who loved the limelight so much that he actually appeared briefly on Broadway. His histrionics on and off the court added to his notoriety as a closet queen. He never openly admitted that he was queer until after he was imprisoned in his fifties and confessed his sexual aberrations in an autobiography.

Tilden was an extremely generous man. He is supposed to have inherited a million dollars and to have made almost a million in tennis, but gave it away or frittered it away in unwise business deals.

They say Tilden may have sent fifty kids through college on scholarships. The only property the guy ever owned, in all the years I knew him, was an automobile, four or five tennis rackets, some kind of a blazer, a pair of slacks and a few sweaters. Everything else he gave away to the kids. He did senseless things. He lived for a while at the Algonquin Hotel in New York City, a rendezvous for writers, actors and others connected with the arts. One time he went to Europe for a couple of months on tour but neglected to check out of the hotel. He had to pay the accumulated rent on his place when he got back. Tilden was a notoriously bad businessman but a fascinating conversationalist. I never tired of talking to Bill. He loved tennis—it was his whole life.

As for lesbians in tennis, if you believe everything you hear, the courts have always been filled with them

154

—and still are. But the same stories circulate about the touring women golf players. And now women runners and jumpers have to undergo sex detection tests before they are accepted in the Olympic Games. I never heard of a woman player—or a woman of any kind— going to jail for sex deviation, so the subject can be dismissed as nothing but hearsay.

I think one reason for the gossip about women tennis players is that so many are tomboy types, whose physical strength or athletic ability turns them on to sport of all kinds. And tennis is one of the sports in which women can get all the exercise they want under highly competitive conditions.

Some tennis players also excelled at other sports. Alice Marble would have made a great baseball player. When Alice was sixteen years old, she could throw a baseball from deep center field in the Seals Stadium in San Francisco and hit home plate. She had a great serve, one of the few really good American twist serves in women's tennis, and a good overhead.

Babe Didrikson, who was a world beater at track and golf, was certainly the tomboy type. She could undoubtedly have become a champion at tennis too, but she did not become interested in the game until she was too old to take it up seriously.

Billie Jean King is another tomboy who could have been a standout in baseball, I'm sure, if women played the game on a large scale. And Margaret Court might have made a good Australian-rules football player.

At the same time, tennis also attracts extremely feminine types—Gussie Moran, young Chris Evert,

Maria Bueno, Valerie Ziegenfuss and, in the old days, Helen Wills and Suzanne Lenglen—all attractive females without anything of the tomboy about them.

On the basis of personal experience and long observation, I am willing to say that the sex lives of tennis players are as normal—if not quite as active or interesting—as those of golfers, baseball players or even pool players.

There are always exceptions—and they make the best gossip items—but the majority of touring tennis players are too busy playing, traveling, packing and unpacking, practicing and doing publicity promotions to do more than think about sex. Except occasionally.

Unlike golfers, for example, tennis players must by definition take care of themselves physically. Very few tennis players smoke cigarettes. And there is no nineteenth hole in tennis. Few tennis players drink anything stronger than beer, and they don't have time to frequent bars where they could pick up girls if the mood is on them. (Usually the mood hit me when I was isolated in a car with two or three other guys, en route to the next one-night stand.)

The schedule of a touring tennis pro is so demanding that he needs to go to bed to *sleep*. Rest is more important than recreation. He is forced into a routine that is basically healthy. It's automatically a Spartan life. A man doesn't have to be a strong self-disciplinarian. I'm not saying that if a sexy dish jumped onto a guy's lap, he'd say, "Nothing doing—I'm in training." But opportunities for sex don't happen that way. You have to go out and make your opportunities. And mostly a player doesn't have the time, even if he has the inclination.

Of course there are exceptions, as we said. I hear that Bob Lutz and Ray Moore, the South African hippie, are pretty good swingers among the younger crop. A few years ago Whitney Reed and Art Larsen, both from the northern California area, which produces more than its share of oddballs, used to stay up all night and manage somehow to play next day.

Tappy Larsen was a bundle of nerves and superstitions and one of the most colorful guys who ever swung a racket. On certain days he would do everything three times—put on shoes and socks three times when dressing—or whatever number was in his mind that day. He never stepped on a line and skipped around the court. He often tapped the court with his racket, which gave rise to the nickname Tappy. He would change the color of his hair a few times during a tournament. He trained on beer but never drank anything stronger. At Wimbledon one year he got the idea that if he dated a different girl each night he would win the title. He missed out one night when a girl stood him up, and he blamed his defeat next day on the date that didn't come off. He was not only a delightful personality but a gifted player, a beautiful stylist. He had complete mastery of the racket. He had all the shots but was not too forceful. He won at Forest Hills in 1950, beating another bundle of nerves, Herb Flam, in five jumpy sets. Larsen's career was cut tragically short soon afterward in a motor-scooter accident that left him permanently disabled.

There were never many real drinkers in tennis, such as you hear about in golf. Walter Hagen, for example, could stay at the nineteenth hole most of the night, take a shower and be on the first tee, ready for a subpar round of golf next morning.

Frank Shields, who was so handsome he had a fling at Hollywood movies, liked parties and drinking. He is supposed to have shown up at Seabright one morning for his match still dressed in the tuxedo he wore to a debutante party the night before. Frank went to Wimbledon one year by boat. The farewell party at Southampton was so lively that he went back to his cabin for a snooze and woke up on his way back to New York.

I often stayed up all night playing poker at the Meadow Club in Southampton, Long Island, during my amateur days. All I needed was a facial massage in the local barber shop to revive me and I could play next morning without sleep. However, I never drank anything stronger than coke. Just one beer was enough to throw off my timing in those days.

The most famous drinking story in tennis concerns Jack Crawford, the Australian with one of the most graceful styles in the history of the game. Crawford arrived in New York in 1933 with three legs of the Grand Slam, having won the Australian, French and Wimbledon titles. He suffered badly from insomnia and was a bundle of nerves by the time he reached the final at Forest Hills against Fred Perry. Like all Aussies, Craw liked an occasional beer but never drank anything stronger. However, on the advice of Vinnie Richards, big Jack took a flask of brandy onto the court and spiked his tea with it during the course of the match. In the fifth set Crawford was so relaxed by the brandy that the Grand Slam didn't mean a thing to him anymore. Perry raced through the set and took the match handily.

You hear a lot of stories these days about the young crop of long-haired hippie-type tennis players. They are supposed to be smoking pot and drinking wine. One American with shoulder-length hair told me he won a major event while absolutely stoned on hashish. A few months later he was at Forest Hills, in the men's locker room, waiting with his partner to go out for their scheduled doubles match. A locker boy asked the player if he wanted a smoke. The player said yes and got stoned again. But this time something went wrong. The kid couldn't focus on the ball, and he and his partner were killed by a team they were supposed to beat easily.

But I would say that the stories about widespread pot smoking are exaggerated. No doubt the kids do it occasionally. But tennis is a game that calls for lots of discipline, hard work and practice. Good players have to take care of themselves physically or they don't last long. There are playboys in tennis today, just as there have always been, but they don't win the big ones.

One of the effects of the tennis explosion now shaking up the game is bound to be the emergence of black players in significant numbers.

Up to now, only two outstanding black players have been developed anywhere in the world. One is Althea Gibson, who started playing paddle tennis in the streets of Harlem, went on to win twice at both Wimbledon and Forest Hills and then gave up tennis for a career as a professional golfer. She is now back in tennis as a teaching pro.

The other is Arthur Ashe, a poor boy from Richmond, Virginia, who had the benefit of early coaching and later exposure to the tennis scene in Southern California and went on to become a Davis Cup star and winner of the first U.S. Open at Forest Hills in 1968. Ashe, a member of Lamar Hunt's World Championship Tennis troupe, has an income in excess of $200,000 a year from prize money, endorsements and other business interests.

That puts Ashe in the same class financially with such highly publicized black stars as Wilt Chamberlain and Kareem Abdul-Jabbar in basketball, or Willie Mays and Hank Aaron in baseball. This has not been lost on the athletic-minded kids in the ghettos. With the example of Ashe before them, they are taking up tennis instead of basketball or baseball, as a potential livelihood as well as a sport they enjoy for its own sake. All they have needed was incentive and opportunity to play the game. Now they are getting the chance through a new junior-development scheme in which Ashe is active and a liberalizing of tennis customs in the South, which formerly excluded young blacks from top competition.

Ashe had two things going for him in tennis—he was exposed to the game early, which is of vital importance, and he was loaded with natural talent. The same was true of Althea, also a fine natural athlete.

Arthur grew up near a Negro playground in Richmond, where his father was the park police officer. Four tennis courts were only a few steps from their home, and Arthur began hitting tennis balls at the age of six with a racket as big as he was. When he was eight, he tried to enter a tournament at a white municipal park but was turned down. When he was ten, Arthur came to the attention of Dr. R. Walter Johnson, a black physician who had a tennis court in his backyard in Lynchburg and whose hobby was encouraging and coaching talented black youngsters in the sport. Althea Gibson had been an earlier protégé of Dr. Johnson's.

Dr. Johnson drilled discipline and deportment into his black boys and girls, teaching them never to show emotion over bad line calls or to argue with umpires. Arthur was his most promising pupil. He did so well in a few white tournaments that Dr. Johnson obtained a scholarship for him at a high school in St. Louis and later at the University of California at Los Angeles. In my opinion, that exposure for four years to the California tennis atmosphere, particularly its high grade of college competition and good coaching, was what turned Arthur into a top-ten player.

His main attribute is his very wiry physique—he hasn't an ounce of fat on him and is as quick about the court as anyone I've ever seen. He has stamina and a high degree of physical fitness. A long match takes very little out of him. The mechanics of his stroke production are sound. He is a hard hitter—Pancho Gonzales thinks he has the hardest, finest serve among the current crop of players. His forehand is not as good as his backhand but is getting better. He is cutting down on his errors and not taking so many chances. A few years ago he had a tendency to overhit—to wallop the ball twice as hard as he needed to win a point. He made a lot of mistakes this way. But he has learned he does not have to do the impossible to win—his natural game is good enough. His judgment is getting better. He has more court know-how. He doesn't run to the net on everything. He's choosing his spots a little better.

His victory over a top field of amateurs and professionals in the first open at Forest Hills was proof that he possesses a first-class talent. Arthur was in the U.S. Army and an amateur when he beat Tom Okker, a Dutch pro, in the finals. Arthur had to be content with silverware as his prize, while Okker pocketed the $14,000 first-prize money. Arthur wasted no time turning pro when he got out of the Army.

There are tremendous outside pressures on Ashe as the first male tennis star of his race, and for a while he did not do too well as a professional. His mind seemed to be on other things and he was not concentrating on playing tennis. Some blacks wanted Arthur to become more political and speak out on the issues of segregation, particularly in sport. He has condemned South Africa's apartheid policy and been banned from playing in that country. However, he feels he can do as much to improve the situation by quiet example. He has gone on a number of State Department-sponsored tours of African countries and has been an inspiration to youngsters there, helping to start wide-scale tennis programs. It has been said that

Arthur may eventually be named United States ambassador to one of those countries.

For all his personal success, Ashe has not forgotten his origins or the ghetto kids who need help to follow his path in tennis. The much-vaunted USLTA junior-development program is more talk than action and it certainly isn't aimed at aiding black slum kids. According to *World Tennis* magazine, money which the USLTA receives for junior development actually goes for general administrative expenses, including the salary of a highly paid executive secretary. The tennis nabobs are only interested in helping the talented (white) youngsters on their Junior Davis Cup and Junior Wightman Cup teams.

Aware of this, Ashe and a few young eastern tennis officials, among them Sherry Snyder and Leif Beck, have formed the National Junior Tennis League and found commercial sponsors, Coca-Cola and Uni-Royal, to finance its operations. The JTL goes right into the core of the inner cities of New York, Philadelphia and elsewhere to start underprivileged kids playing in organized league competition. The theme is instant competition. To get the boys and girls interested in the game they are given the chance to compete in regular challenge matches and team matches, long before they learn all the strokes. Arthur believes that, in order to draw kids away from baseball, basketball and other team sports, you must offer them this kind of immediate action.

The JTL also supplies rackets, balls and colored uniforms. Explains Arthur, "A uniform gives a kid a

163

sense of identity as a team member and makes tennis more like other sports"—he is against the all-white tradition of dress for the kids and for himself.

The JTL also starts the kids off with a simplified scoring system, 1–2–3–4 and so forth, up to thirty-one points a game, as in Ping-Pong. Ashe believes that once a kid is hooked on tennis this way, it is easy to teach him the fifteen-thirty-forty-deuce scoring which will probably never be changed, despite the efforts of reformers such as Jimmy Van Alen of Newport who want to take "love" out of tennis and modernize its scoring method.

Realistically, Arthur feels that only a minority of underprivileged kids can be swung over to tennis. "If ten percent of the kids you start with continue playing, that's good." Given the great love and natural aptitude of black children for all kinds of sports, that's enough of a percentage to produce future champions.

The time is overdue for the arrival of many fine black players on the tennis scene. Now that television is bringing top tennis to the mass viewing public on a regular basis, black youngsters can dream of becoming an Arthur Ashe as they once yearned to be a Willie Mays or a Wilt Chamberlain.

9

IT'S IRONIC that Wimbledon, which pioneered open tennis and first admitted professionals in 1968, has had nothing but trouble with the pros ever since. As a result of a series of quarrrels with the top tennis promoter, Lamar Hunt of Texas, and his World Championship Tennis troupe, and then with the players' union, the Association of Tennis Players, Wimbledon lost the world's top men players beginning in 1972. In that year Rod Laver, the game's top money winner, and a number of other WCT stars shunned Wimbledon. In 1973 more than seventy members of the ATP, including defending champion Stan Smith and most of the name players, boycotted Wimbledon. It became a kind of ghost tournament as far as the men were concerned. The 1973 winner, Jan Kodes of Czechoslovakia, who beat Alex Metreveli of Russia in a boring final, lacked the prestige that used to go along with being the Wimbledon champion.

At the root of Wimbledon's troubles is a power struggle between the players, who are now rolling in money and want a lot more to say about when and where and who they play, and the Old Guard tennis associations in the various countries, who are desperately trying to retain control of the sport. The players no longer need to play at Wimbledon and Forest Hills in order to make a name for themselves and cash in on it. They can make all the money they need on the million-dollar WCT circuit, or on the so-called independent circuit sponsored by the USLTA each winter, or on the international Grand Prix circuit. As a result, the tennis associations are losing control of their players, who now refuse to play on Davis Cup teams, for example, if this interferes with their prize money.

This is what lay behind the 1973 mass boycott of Wimbledon. Nikki Pilic of Yugoslavia, a WCT player, ignored his country's request to play a Davis Cup match in Belgrade. Instead Pilic played in the Alan King Classic in Las Vegas, where $130,000 in prize money was up for grabs. Thereupon the Yugoslav Tennis Association suspended Pilic for three months, a punishment upheld by the International Lawn Tennis Federation, the world governing body of the sport. Wimbledon upheld the suspension and refused to accept Pilic's entry.

The ATP decided to force a showdown over the Pilic issue. This players' union, which is headed by Cliff Drysdale of South Africa, has called on Jack Kramer to act as unpaid executive director. Jack, my old companion on the pro tour, seems to pop up everywhere in tennis these days. He is well fixed financially and can devote himself mainly to tennis affairs. Although he once warred with the tennis establishment,

166

Jack is now an official of the Southern California Association and is tournament director of Perry Jones's old pet project, the Pacific Southwest Championships in LA. Jack has retained the respect of the players despite his official status. The ATP ordered its members to boycott Wimbledon because of Pilic's suspension. All but three ATP members obeyed the boycott. They were Ilie Nastase of Romania, who explained that his Communist country had ordered him to play, Ray Keldie, a young Australian, and Roger Taylor, an Englishman who yielded to pressures to play in his country's biggest tennis spectacle. Naturally the other ATP members resented the actions of these three, and there was a lot of talk of fining them or taking some other kind of action against them.

Although the absence of Smith, Laver, Rosewall, Ashe and the other top stars did not hurt the attendance at Wimbledon—which was sold out months before the boycott occurred—it reduced it to a second-rate men's tournament. Not even Wimbledon, with all its traditions and prestige, can afford this downgrading in quality. Some kind of compromise will have to be worked out between Wimbledon, the ILTF, and the players. What Kramer and the ATP are seeking is a new International Tennis Council, in which the players will have an equal voice with the ILTF, Wimbledon and other major tournaments and tournament sponsors.

Another threat to Wimbledon has come from the new World Team Tennis League, which is trying to sign the top sixty-four men and women players to form individual teams representing sixteen American cities. The league intends to start operating in May 1974, following the WCT finals in Dallas and the end of that group's season. The WCT would then begin a three-month series of intercity team matches which would carry on right through the Italian, French and Wimbledon tournaments. WTT is headed by Larry King, the husband of Billie Jean, and backed by a group of wealthy sports promoters. It is in a position to make the top players, both men and women, a series of financial offers they can't refuse. One English newspaper warned that the WTT intended to "drive another nail into Wimbledon's coffin."

Americans were not very popular at Wimbledon following the boycott. English sports commentators accused the ATP of trying to wreck Wimbledon, and Jack Kramer became the archvillain. Kramer was always well liked at Wimbledon and as an ex-champion was something of a hero. But his name suddenly became a dirty word to the English, and the BBC forced Jack out of his long-time job as TV commentator for the Wimbledon matches.

My sympathies are with the players, who have obviously outgrown the ILTF, the USLTA and the other national tennis associations. They were set up a hundred years ago to administer amateur tennis and have no business trying to run pro tennis, which is now bursting at the seams.

The men who run tennis lack the imagination and the business experience to deal with sports promoters, such as Lamar Hunt, and the commercial sponsors and television networks who now play such a big part in the world of professional tennis.

Lamar Hunt, in my opinion, has done more for pro tennis and pro tennis players than anybody else who has ever come into the game. He used his enormous wealth and experience in pro football and other sports to set up a permanent pro tennis circuit, with sixty-four players on a guaranteed annual income of $12,000 a year minimum, playing for $1 million prize money. He has set new standards of promoting which are a far cry from my days of helter-skelter one-night stands.

But in so doing, Hunt stepped on the toes of amateur tennis officials. They were afraid that his streamlined business operations would put him in control of the entire game and push the tennis associations into the background, with the badge wearers relegated to the role of figureheads.

Hunt is the son of H. L. Hunt, a Texas tycoon who made his money in oil and cattle. When Lamar set out to form the American Football League, a friend went to H. L. and warned him, "Your boy is going to lose a million dollars a year."

"Well," the old man replied, "then he's only got a hundred years to go."

H. L. Hunt is probably one of the two or three richest men in the world, right up there with Paul Getty and Howard Hughes. The Hunt family, the old man and his sons and sons-in-law, occupy nine floors of a skyscraper in Dallas, where they direct a worldwide empire in oil, cattle, real estate and thoroughbred racehorse breeding. This Hunt complex is said to generate a million dollars a day in income.

Lamar Hunt's special province is professional

sports. He owns the Kansas City Chiefs football team and has an interest in a Texas League baseball team and a professional soccer team. But sports are his business, not his hobby. He is out to make money with his teams, including the WCT tennis group, which showed a financial profit after three years in business.

I once had the opportunity of telling Hunt what a tremendous thing he was doing for the players. I have been a tennis promoter, but my heart really is in playing the game. Still, as a player, I appreciate what he has done.

Back in 1963, when pro tennis was in the doldrums, Ken Rosewall and Rod Laver battled through to the finals of the pro tournament at Forest Hills. The tennis was great but the crowds were not. The two young, inexperienced promoters who staged the tournament went broke doing so. The result was that neither Rosewall, the winner, nor Laver, the runner-up, ever got a nickel out of the tournament.

By contrast, the same two players contested the finals of the first World Championship of Tennis, the climax of the Hunt group's tour, in Dallas, eight years later, in November of 1971, and collected handsomely.

Rosewall, the winner, picked up a check for $50,000—at that time the biggest single payoff in tennis history, plus a $4,000 sports car and a diamond ring. Laver, again the runner-up, got a check for $20,000. That brought Rod's money winnings for the year to $292,717. More impressive still, it made Rod the first tennis millionaire, with career earnings of $1,007,000 in his nine years as a pro. Thanks to Lamar Hunt, Rod earned more money, $290,000 in

1971, than the top pro golfer, Jack Nicklaus, who garnered a mere $235,000.

Lamar Hunt's players won the grand total of $1,518,000 during 1971. Still Hunt was able to finish the year in the black. And this was accomplished without television sponsorship. But beginning early in 1972, the National Broadcasting Company began nationwide telecasting of the Sunday finals of the WCT tour. It was the first time tennis had ever received continuous coverage in this country by a commercial network. The advertisers and the sponsors had discovered the tennis audience as a tremendous new market for their wares.

The counterpart of Lamar Hunt in women's pro tennis is Gladys Heldman, a dynamic, no-nonsense businesswoman. She is single-handedly responsible for the birth of a separate pro tour for women players.

Mrs. Heldman has a lifelong tennis background. She is married to Julius Heldman, a research chemist who grew up in my old hometown, LA, and was once National Junior Tennis Champion. Their daughter, Julie, is one of the top ten women players in the country.

A former tournament player herself, Mrs. Heldman started *World Tennis* magazine in back of a laundry in New York twenty-odd years ago and made it the most successful and influential publication in tennis history. She sold the magazine to CBS recently for a reported sum of $2 million but continues as publisher with full control of its editorial policies. Those policies through the years have been mainly anti-Establishment. She has warred with the USLTA officials from the very beginning, always taking the part of the players in their squabbles with the tennis brass.

She supported Billie Jean King and the other women players who refused to play in the Pacific Southwest Championships a few years ago because of the low prize money Jack Kramer was offering them. Mrs. Heldman announced that, instead of playing the Pacific Southwest, the rebels would play in the first women's pro tournament, to be sponsored by *World Tennis* magazine. That first tournament, held in the face of USLTA disapproval, eventually spread into a full-scale women's pro circuit. This was made possible by the commercial sponsorship of Virginia Slims cigarettes, whose motto is "You've come a long way, baby." It is an apt one for the women pros, who are now playing for total prize money of $850,000 a year on a circuit taking in twenty-two cities. Billie Jean King, a Virginia Slims player, has earned more than $100,000 a year for the past two years, making her the best-paid woman athlete in sports history.

I think the secret of their success is that the women have set up their own separate pro circuit, just like the women golfers. I don't like men and women playing in the same tournaments. They each do better on their own.

10

MY VICTORY over Margaret Court established me as the Jane L. Sullivan of tennis. I won that title by a knock-out blow, before the largest audience that ever watched a tennis match. From now on I want to give all contenders for my title a crack at me. At the moment I envision a series of challenge matches, six months or so apart, first against Billie Jean King, then Chris Evert, Evonne Goolagong and anyone else who qualifies by winning the big tournaments. I would be delighted to give Margaret Court a return match, perhaps Down Under, with the Pacific satellite beaming the action to North America and Europe and wherever else TV can go in the world. The stakes for all my matches from now on will be ten times what they were at San Diego—at least $100,000, thanks to television sponsors and my new business agent, Jerry Perenchio. Jerry was the mastermind behind the $20 million bout between Muhammad Ali and Joe Frazier. Jerry thinks big and has big ideas for me, particularly on television.

Jerry got interested in promoting my future

matches when he watched the Court-Riggs spectacular on television. "When it came on," he told me, "the whole town stopped. Everyone was turned on by the match. Women bet on Margaret Court. Men bet on Bobby Riggs. And I said to myself, 'This isn't tennis— it's something bigger.' "

Jerry called a press conference at the Town Tennis Club in New York to announce that Billie Jean King had agreed to play me at a time and place to be announced for $100,000—winner-take-all.

"The Ali-Frazier fight was 'the Fight,' " Jerry told the huge turnout of reporters, radio and TV broadcasters. "This is 'the Match.' "

The media coverage of that conference was the greatest since the Ali-Frazier fight. The sports reporters called me "the white Muhammad Ali," with a gift of gab to match that of the former world champion. But Billie Jean, who can talk as long and loud and fast as I can, was a match for me face to face.

"You do your hustling off the court," she told me in our confrontation before the microphones. "I'll do my hustling on the court."

My prematch plan for Billie Jean was the same as the one I used against Margaret Court. I intended to put the pressure on her from the very beginning and keep building it up.

"This is the Libber versus the Lobber," I told the press conference. "We said we had the Match of the Century the last time. But obviously we had the wrong girl. We should have had the Women's Lib leader, Billie Jean.

"If there was a lot of pressure on Margaret Court,

can you imagine how much pressure there will be on Billie Jean King when she goes out on the court against me? I wonder if she'll even show up."

Billie Jean's response was that Margaret had collapsed under the strain because of her temperament. "I would have given her five beers and a couple of aspirins before the match to calm her down," Billie Jean said. "But I'm different. I like pressure as much as Riggs does."

The women reporters at the conference apparently agreed with everything she said. They stormed up to me afterward. Nora Ephron of *Esquire* magazine, a prime mover in the Women's Lib movement, said, "Bobby, we've got five hundred dollars to bet against you, will you cover it?"

"Is this jawboning or whipout?" I asked. "Let's see the color of your money."

She showed me a fistful of bills collected from the women reporters.

"But we want odds of eight to five," she added. "That's Jimmy the Greek's line in Las Vegas."

I protested that the match was no more than an even-money bet, the same as Court-Riggs, but Nora stood firm for 8-to-5 odds.

"Okay," I said finally. "You're gonna blow your dough anyway—what's the difference what the odds are?"

This show of loyalty by the women reporters toward Billie Jean was something new for a press conference. The press is notoriously shy of putting up money to *see* a sports contest, much less to bet on one. But as Jerry Perenchio said, this whole business of man versus woman, youth versus age, transcends sports.

Incidentally, Gene Scott, a top New York player in his midthirties who had once played Billie Jean, attended the conference. He tried, without success, to straighten out the women reporters.

"Women tennis players can't stand the pressure of playing against men," he told them. "Girls are brought up from the time they are six to read books, eat candy and go to dancing class. They can't compete against men, can't stand the strain."

Scott played Billie Jean in an exhibition during an indoor tournament at C. W. Post College on Long Island. He spotted her ten points in a twenty-one-point VASSS match and won twenty-one to seventeen. What happened, a reporter asked. "She choked," Scott replied.

I figured that my win over Margaret Court, plus the challenge from Billie Jean, entitled me to play in women's tournaments. "Everyone knows that sex doesn't matter after fifty-five," I said in submitting my entry to the Virginia Slims tournament at Newport. Jimmy Van Alen, the tournament director, said I'd have to pass a medical test first. If he was thinking in terms of an operation in Denmark, I draw the line. I won't go that route. When eighty of the top men pros pulled out of Wimbledon, I demanded that I be allowed to play in the women's event. My idea was to breathe a little life into a ghost tournament, but Mike Gibson, the tournament chairman at Wimbledon, didn't buy it.

In addition to playing challenges against women, I want to travel around the country staging handicap matches against local players. At Tehachapi, California, I came out on a court dressed in an ankle-length fireman's raincoat, boots up to my knees and carrying a suitcase in my left hand. Terry Reagan, president of the Dart Industries land development division, was my opponent. He wore a tennis dress and a red woman's wig, à la Margaret Court. Terry is a good player and I had my hands full—literally—beating him with my handicap. The crowd loved the show. I was allowed to bounce the ball on serving and got so much spin on it that way that I could make all kinds of weird shots. I'd like to work up an act using trick shots, something like Joe Kirkwood and Ed Hahn used to do in golf.

If the odds are right, I'd be willing to play anything; it doesn't have to be tennis. On the Mike Wallace show the camera followed me around Las Vegas, showing a typical day in the life of Bobby Riggs. I bumped into Joe Louis and challenged him to a contest on the putting green. I shot baskets with the Van Arsdale brothers. I played tennis against Steve Lawrence and Paul Anka at the same time, with eight chairs on my side of the net, carrying a suitcase and receiving serve sitting down. I pitched cards into a hat against tennis pro Lornie Kuhle, for a sizable bet. After that I played backgammon with Ray Moore, the South African with the longest hair in tennis, ending with a poker session with Art Tilton, a California tennis pro.

The Court match made me an instant celebrity. Wherever I go, people ask for my autograph. Oddly enough, many women come up to shake hands with me, despite my unofficial title of male chauvinist number one. Taxi drivers know me right away. "I never saw a tennis match in my life," one cabbie told me in New York, "but I watched you play that big dame from Australia. Great."

When I drive along the LA freeway, guys come up alongside, honk their horns and raise their fists in a victory salute: "Attaboy, Bobby." The other day I saw a bumper sticker: "Bobby Riggs for President."

Sports Illustrated magazine came out a few days after the big match with my picture on the cover, bearing the caption "Never bet against this man." That warning has become something of a trademark. (It has also hampered my negotiations in man-to-man betting.) Bloomingdale's department store in New York ran a seies of advertisements for tennis gear, showing a player in dark-rimmed glasses with a white visor like the one I wore against Margaret. The first ad was captioned "Never bet against this man" but didn't further identify him. It wasn't necessary. One of my kids even thought I had posed for the ads.

I was astonished at the recognition I got from baseball fans at Shea Stadium when I was guest announcer with Curt Gowdy and Tony Kubek on the NBC Monday Night Baseball Program. One group of fans came in with a big sign, "Riggs versus Secretariat 2 to 5." I guess that was supposed to be the odds on me to run against the wonder horse. Another sign read "Mahwah Loves Bobby Riggs." I didn't even know there was a place called Mahwah—it's in New Jersey somewhere—much less that I had admirers there. Randy Moffett, who is Billie Jean King's brother, pitched for the Giants at the end of their game against the Mets. I asked him how he thought Billie Jean would do against me. "I've got to like my sister," he replied. I must remember to get in touch with Randy before I play Billie Jean.

It was all pretty heady stuff for an old guy who had been out of the limelight for twenty-five years—and was never much of a celebrity even as world tennis champion.

"It's like being reincarnated," I told sports writer Will Grimsley, an old friend who knew me when. "This is the greatest thing I've ever done, bigger than Wimbledon or Forest Hills, bigger than winning the pro tour. This is the highlight of my career."

I was deluged with money offers for everything from endorsing dog food (because I have played with a poodle on a string?) to baby bottles (because I beat a mother?). I was invited to play a guest shot on *All in the Family*, as the male chauvinist friend of Archie Bunker. Some company wanted to bring out a Bobby Riggs watch, along the lines of the Mickey Mouse gadgets, with the dial bearing the letters MCC (male chauvinist champion) and showing me with one foot in the grave. Every vitamin manufacturer in the world wanted to get me to endorse their pills when they heard about my daily diet of 415.

Major hotel chains, including Holiday Inns and Hilton, wanted to make me their tennis director. Linda Tuero, tenth-ranking woman in the world, asked me to give her lessons; "You know how to beat these girls, how about teaching me?" A girl at the Las Vegas Country Club offered to pay me $100 an hour for a series of lessons.

After my appearance with Don Rickles, substitute host on the Johnny Carson night program, every TV talk show in the country got in touch with me. Rickles, who is a hard man to top, admitted I had outtalked him.

Mickey Rooney, who bears a resemblance to me, telephoned to say, "I want to play you in the movies." I replied, "The hell you do—I'll play myself." A Hollywood studio has actually approached me to do my life story.

My mailman at Newport Beach, California, developed tennis elbow from lugging in bundles of letters. Most of them were from men congratulating me for upholding the banner of male supremacy. A lot of them urged me to go on playing women. One guy said I should play Chris Evert and bill the match as Beauty and the Beast.

The match proved a real shot in the arm for senior tennis, as I hoped it would. Alvin Bunis, a retired Cincinnati businessman, announced soon afterward that he had put together a Grand Masters tournament circuit with $250,000 in prize money for old gaffers such as Frank Sedgman, Jaroslav Drobny, Frankie Parker, Gardnar Mulloy, Vic Seixas, Pancho Segura and myself. The Grand Masters will tour ten cities in the United States and Europe. They hope to draw crowds of middle-aged fans who can relate to them better than they can to the Smiths and the other young stars.

"Senior tennis is a thinking man's game," said Bunis. I couldn't agree more. He added, "Watching the Grand Masters under tournament conditions will be like taking lessons from the finest teachers of the game."

Imitation is supposed to be the sincerest form of flattery. In that case I was certainly flattered by Jimmy Demaret, the golfer, and by Amarillo Slim, the highly touted poker player. Demaret tried to get into my act by issuing a challenge to Kathy Whitworth, the leading money winner on the women's professional golf tour, to a winner-take-all match. Jimmy, fifty-eight, is even older than I am. But in golf age doesn't mean as much as it does in tennis. Sammy Snead, who is well into his sixties, is still making plenty on the men's pro tour and would be a dead cinch to beat Demaret, who is retired from the tour, as well as every woman in the world. I liked one crack of Demaret's: "Women want their liberation—let's liberate them from their money!"

As for Amarillo Slim, he announced in Las Vegas that he was prepared to tutor a woman to take me on at poker. Slim was trying to cash in on my publicity by declaring, wrongly, that I had challenged him to produce a woman poker player as my next opponent. But if Slim means it and will put up the prize money I'll take on his wonder woman. Card games are not my strong suit—I like more control over the game than I get at cards or casino gambling —but I like a challenge, especially when someone else is putting up the money.

At Madison Square Garden during a track meet, a 250-pound shot-putter ran a sixty-yard dash against a girl sprinter—and beat her.

181

Someone claiming to be the world woman rodeo champion challenged me to a goat-roping contest for a winner-take-all stake of $10,000. She offered to spot me a five-second handicap. I wired back, "NOT MUCH EXPERIENCE AT GOAT-ROPING BUT HAPPY TO ACCEPT CHALLENGE. FIRST, NEED TIME TO PRACTICE. SECONDLY, WANT $25,000 PRIZE NOT $10,000. THIRDLY, WANT TEN SECONDS HANDICAP NOT FIVE." I never got a reply.

At the Los Angeles Tennis Club, my old stamping ground, three good woman players, Tory Fretz, who is on the Virginia Slims circuit, Laurie Tenney and Stephanie Grant challenged three older men and beat them in both singles and doubles matches.

In Chicago, a group of woman bowlers challenged the men in their academy to a team match. The women got beaten.

At Princeton University the women's varsity tennis team's star player. Marjory Gengler, who is unbeaten in college competition, challenged Jeff Oakes, a member of the men's junior varsity team. Three of her teammates also challenged three other men's JV players. It was quite an occasion, with no less an umpire than Stan Smith in the chair and hundreds of students in the stands. The *Daily Princetonian* reported, "Except for the absence of television coverage, the 4–0 win for the men's JV over the women's varsity outclassed Riggs' production in every category." Oh, yeah?

In Philadelphia, Mrs. Karen Constant, who won the women's national sculling title ten times, challenged Jack Kelly, Jr., former Olympic and Diamond Scull winner, to a 1,500-meter race. She felt the image of women athletes had been dealt a severe blow when I beat Margaret Court and wanted to wipe out the stigma. Mrs. Constant, who is twenty-nine, said her husband would put up $5,000 in prize money if Kelly, who is forty-six, would row against her. Jack, brother of Princess Grace of Monaco, the ex-movie star, said he would accept Mrs. Constant's challenge if he could "get some time off in the evenings to train." I like Jack's spirit and might have a few bucks on him if he takes on the women's champ.

Instant fame has done a lot to improve my social life. As a divorced man, constantly on the go, I have been getting the red-carpet treatment, especially from the opposite sex. At one senior tournament I was offered dates with any of the three most eligible girls— the richest, the prettiest or the biggest swinger. "Which way do you want to go?" they asked me.

But if a girl gets serious, wants the lifetime franchise, an exclusive deal, I can't go for that. I'm not ready to block out all the other action.

I have decided I'm not cut out for marriage. I was married twice, once for thirteen years and again for twenty years. I went through the motions of being a husband and a father. I've got six kids. I love them all and I know they love me. But my heart wasn't in the home. It was really out there on the tennis court or the golf course or at the gin-rummy table.

My first divorce, as I said, was simply the result of prolonged absences, but I'm happy to say that my relationship with Kay is still warm and cordial. After the Court match, I got a telegram from her saying,

"You're still the greatest." Bobby and Larry are also close to their mother, who has remarried.

My second wife, Priscilla, was 100 percent dedicated and did everything possible to make a fine home for me and our four children, John, Jimmy, Dolly and Billy, when they were growing up. But I was anything but the ideal husband and father. I was not the kind of father who would gather the kids together on a Saturday and take them to Jones Beach, or out somewhere for a picnic. I was too self-centered, to absorbed in my games and betting to realize my potential as a father, husband or businessman. Although I was an executive in Priscilla's family business, I never really tried to get to the top in it. I had no desire to make it big in the business world.

Priscilla never really understood my compulsion to bet on myself. "Bobby, you don't need to win five hundred dollars on a game," she would say. "Can't you get it through your head that you're a millionaire? Don't you realize that half of what I've got belongs to you?"

But I never accepted that. I told her, "What you've got is yours. Only what I've earned is mine."

I have always been a great reader of the sports pages and keep up with all sports as well as my own. Priscilla never looked at the sports pages. She didn't even know the names of the pro football teams. I would watch all four football games on TV on New Year's Day and have bets on all of them. Priscilla didn't even come into the room. She frowns on card games, backgammon, in fact all forms of gambling, because of her strong religious background. I had a similar background but it didn't lessen my love for gambling. Religion was one of the few things that Priscilla and I had in common. My Sunday school lessons were short on biblical references but long on inspirational messages drawn from my experiences in sports. The kids also learned a few things about figuring odds, which wasn't in the curriculum.

As the years went by, I was spending more and more time playing money matches at the Tennis Center in New York City or golf at the Plandome Club near our home or gin rummy in the men's locker room. When the kids had all left home, either to get married or to attend school and college, Priscilla finally took the initiative.

"Bobby, you need me like you need a hole in the head," she said. "I'll always love you. But you have so many friends and so many outside interests you don't really need me."

Our divorce in 1972 was friendly. I left the family business, and with my stock holdings and other financial arrangements I was able to retire comfortably in California. I remain on the best of terms with Priscilla and with our four children.

My only disappointment is that none of my children, with the exception of Larry, ever took up tennis seriously. Larry is a better-than-average club player who makes his living as a stock broker in LA.

As far as the future is concerned, I'm going to continue my vitamin program. I think it is going to lengthen my life span. I believe what Rheo Blair has told me—that if I stay on this program I'll live to at least ninety-eight or ninety-nine.

I expect to reach one hundred. I expect to be playing very good tennis up to seventy-five or eighty. I plan to go and play in these fifty-five-and-over, sixty-and-over, sixty-five-and-over, seventy-and-over, seventy-five-and-over tournaments. I'd like to be like the late King of Sweden, whom I played with and knew quite well. He played tennis until he was ninety.

As the world's women's champion, I want to play the woman challenger of the year every year until I'm beaten. I figure that I've got another ten years left of beating women players—until I'm sixty-five.

This is my idea of paradise—to be able to keep on playing good tennis. I want always to be the best player in the world for my age. I always was the best player in the world for my age, ever since I was twelve. I was the best twelve-year-old player in the world, the best thirteen-, the best fourteen-, fifteen-, sixteen-, seventeen-, eighteen-year-old player. There has never been a year that anybody was better at my exact age.

It took me a long time to catch up with Don Budge, but he was three years older. And of course there were always guys who were younger, like Rod Laver and hundreds of guys now, who were better.

But I am still the best player in the world for my age. My goal is to continue to be able to make that claim.

I have put in my will that I want to be cremated. I want to have one half of my ashes spread over the stadium court at Forest Hills and half over the center court at the Los Angeles Tennis Club, where I grew up and played so many matches. I figure that should be in the year 2018, roughly 6,750,000 pills from now.

Appendix:
Airtight Tennis

AIRTIGHT TENNIS is tennis without holes, tennis without errors. It's defensive tennis. It's keeping the ball everlastingly in play. It's letting the opponent make all the errors. It's Riggs-type tennis. It's the kind of retrieving tennis I've always played. And now that I'm middle-aged I find it's the kind of tennis which is also best suited to the ordinary weekend player, the club player, the player who never won a tournament trophy and never will.

Airtight tennis is the game for everyone, regardless of age or sex, who wants to win but wants to get all the fun possible out of playing the game as well. After all, you go out on a tennis court to hit balls. You'll hit a million of them when you play airtight tennis.

The tennis explosion of the past few years shook up the forty-and-over population more than any other. Our doctors gave us the go-ahead signal to engage in strenuous sports. They told us that playing two sets of tennis on a Sunday afternoon was better for our hearts than two hours of cocktails.

In airtight tennis you keep your errors to an absolute minimum. You let the other fellow make the mistakes. In ordinary social tennis, played by the average person, 95 percent of the matches are won by the defensive player, not the slam-bang attacker with the big serve—which goes out more than it goes in.

In simple language, airtight tennis means not trying foolish shots. Stay with the shots you know you can make. There is no point to banging the ball around or trying to hit it harder than necessary.

Say to yourself, "I'm going to concentrate. I'm going to keep my eye on the ball. I'm going to get to the ball early. I'm going to hit back safe and sure. I'm going to force this guy into playing dangerously. Let him hit harder. Let him try to end a rally. I'll just keep plugging away, getting the ball back."

Many players make the mistake of trying to do more than they can with the ball. They want to copy Stan Smith or Rod Laver or Pancho Gonzales. They want to *look* good. They'd rather miss five shots, hit as hard as possible, than make one sure shot, hit softly. This kind of play will never make you a winner.

I have always wanted to win, regardless of how I looked taking a point. I happen to have a good style but I have never been vain about it. I have always played cautiously. I have always *aimed* the ball. I once went six months in tournament competition as an amateur without double-faulting. I have always played percentage tennis and let the glamour boys impress the galleries.

Let's face it: the most glamorous part of any game is the offense. However, the defense is almost always the key to victory. The reason the New York Knickerbockers became world basketball champions in 1973 was because they were a better defensive team than the Los Angeles Lakers, the runners-up. The Lakers made the mistake of trying to outdefense the Knicks instead of playing their own high-scoring game. They fell into a trap because the Knicks were much better defenders.

In football, George Allen has compiled a great record with the Washington Redskins by making them the best defensive team in the country. My theory, that the defense is more important than the offense, has never been endorsed by the so-called experts. They point to the big serve of Jack Kramer and Pancho Gonzales as if that was the key to their success. Actually, Kramer had extremely sound ground strokes and Gonzales is primarily a defensive player. The public doesn't realize this. Gonzales has a catchy volley, not a punchy putaway shot. He sticks his racket out and catches the ball, making a dink shot or a drop volley out of it. Pancho looks impressive as he pounds his serve and overheads. But the thing that made him great, in my opinion, was his ability to use defensive tactics. He could run and stretch and reach and make incredible gets and saves.

The best defensive players are usually short men— Pancho Segura, Ken Rosewall, Art Larsen and me. All of us had basically sound ground strokes and were originally back-court players. However, in big-time tennis you can't stick to the baseline. You've got to come to net for the volley and overhead. Rosewall never became a great player until he realized the strength of the net position. He discovered this when he was playing Lew Hoad in the singles final at Forest Hills in 1956. Lew had three legs on the Grand Slam and took the first set from Ken. Ken knew instinctively that he had to change his game if he was going to beat Hoad on the fast grass surface. He is a very good volleyer who never felt at home at the net. But he started to come in behind his serve in the second set and turned it around, beating Lew in four sets. Ken has become as good a net-rusher as anybody in the game, but basically he is a defensive player with a truly great return of service.

A defensive player has got to be a good court coverer. He must be able to anticipate where the ball is going and start for it as soon as possible. He must stay on his toes, literally, and be ready to take off in any direction as soon as his opponent hits the ball.

Ball control is all-important in airtight tennis. Hit your shots easily and fluently, with a good follow-through. Keep your eye on the ball—all the way. Many people make the mistake of watching the ball as it comes to them and then taking their eyes off it at the last moment to see where the opponent is. You should look at your opponent as he hits the ball but not again until you have actually seen the ball touch the strings on your racket. You should be thinking *where* you want to hit the ball as you wait for it to get to you. Then *aim* it at the right spot.

The older player should try to conserve his energy. That means not running after shots that are obviously out of reach—and not running for a loose ball that has rolled into a neighboring court. If you are playing doubles, let your partner chase the balls, especially if he is younger than you are.

Know yourself and your limitations. Don't waste your time and energy on flashy shots. Wait for the opportunity to use your best shot—a cross-court forehand or a backhand down the line. Don't try to make a shot when you are out of position. Wait for the right moment. Don't try for winners on every shot. Don't forget most points are the result of errors. Let your opponent make them.

Vary your shots. The weekend player's big mistake is hitting every ball with the same speed—usually as hard as he can. Mix up your shots and you'll mix up your opponent. Give him a hard drive into the corner, then try a soft cross-court to bring him forward. Lob him. Give him a semilob to his backhand. Don't hit every ball the same way. Hit some short, some deep. Hit a flat ball, then put spin on the next one. Keep your opponent guessing. Never let him get into a groove against your shots. Try to break up the rhythm of his game. Keep him off balance. Even if you can hit a hard, safe ball, vary it occasionally with spin. Change the pace of your ball. Variety is the spice of airtight tennis.

Always try to prevent your opponent from playing his game. If he is a slugger, give him nothing to hit but junk balls, slow stuff, dinks and drop shots. If he is a net-rusher, lob him. Keep the ball away from his strong side. When I played Don Budge, who had probably the best backhand ever, I hit to his forehand most of the time. But there is a danger here, too. You can improve an opponent's weak side if you concentrate on it by hitting every shot to that side. So you have to vary your pattern and occasionally go to his strong side.

In my match against Margaret Court I constantly varied my shots. It's hard for anybody to make a forceful shot off a semilob that lands six feet behind the service line and two or three feet from the baseline. This ball will bounce high to the backhand unless the opponent sees it coming very early and runs to net to volley it. It's not a dazzling offensive play but it wins points. Margaret chose to let this shot bounce, and she couldn't do anything but hit it right back to me. My next shot would be to her forehand, then a high floating lob again. I was giving her balls with spin and without spin. I concentrated on shots that she could not attack on. She wanted to be aggressive, forceful, but my junk shots frustrated her.

In airtight tennis, it is important to play to the score, thinking beyond the point being played.

For example, you're down 1–4 in the first set of a match and you're in trouble. If you play evenly from there on, the set would go to your opponent, 6 to 3. That doesn't help you at all. Why not try to change the rhythm, the timing of the set, a little bit, do something to disconcert the opponent? Here's where a bit of gamesmanship comes in. Take some chances; try to make the opponent work as much as possible; be a little reckless, because the set is virtually gone anyhow. You really don't care whether or not you make the shot, so take your racket back and try to cream a return of serve. It might come off. Or you can make a sacrifice shot, a drop shot, or a lob that chases him back to the baseline. Make your opponent run around the court, make him work for every point, even though he's winning each game and takes the set 6 to 1.

You get what you want—to serve first in the second set. And your opponent is a bit cocky, a bit overconfident, and lets down a bit. You jump out to a good start in the second set and you might have a 3–0 or 3–1 lead. Even though he's won more games than you have in the first set, that set is erased. The three games you won in the second set have given you the lead and you're back in the match. That comes from thinking ahead in the first set, when you were down, and playing to the score.

Another situation which can come up is when you are at 5 to 5 and 40–love in your opponent's favor. Now you do something daring—like taking the serve on the rise and driving it into a corner instead of trying to play a safe return. If the shot comes off, you try something else, something different. Change the pattern of play. If you can get the score to deuce, it's anyone's set. Your opponent is very discouraged at letting you off the hook.

Learning how to play to the score comes only with lots of experience. It's really for the more seasoned player, who comes to know when to play hard, when to let up and when to make the sacrifice plays.

And remember this cardinal rule: Never change a winning game; always change a losing game.

If you are in a losing position, down a set or down two or three games, it's time for a change.

If you are in a leading position, stay with your game plan, with your successful tactics. Never make the mistake of playing your opponent's game if yours is working.

SERVING

I'd like to give you a few tips on serving. The average player should try just to get the ball across the net and into the box—in other words, get it into play. If he can get a nice little spin on the serve, beautiful. With the right grip, he should be able to place the ball, hit it into the backhand corner or down the middle. He might also try to learn to hit a sidespin serve to the forehand. Most people make the mistake of trying to hit the first ball too hard and the second ball too soft. You should develop a dependable first serve and a medium-paced second serve.

But you must strive to get your first serve in. This is even more important in doubles than in singles. This is a

192

key tactic. You don't even have to serve so well in doubles, where you have a partner at the net to block off half the court. You don't want your opponent to get set for a second serve. Keep him guessing where you will put your first serve. I can't overemphasize, in singles or doubles, how important it is to get a high percentage of first serves in.

The secret of great tennis, championship variety, is controlled speed. The top players can hit the ball very hard, but with them it's not risky, it's a safe shot, played well within their framework. They can hit the first serve like a bullet and still make good on 70 percent of them. It's okay for them to hit that hard because they also have a very good second serve if they don't get the first in. But the weekend player cannot afford to hit his serve as hard as he can. Moderation is the key to a good first and second serve.

The serve is one shot you can work on by yourself. The way to improve is to get a big basket of balls, go out on the court, and hit to targets set up in the opposite service boxes. Put an old inner tube on the center line where it connects with the service line, so that it spills over into the forehand receiving box and the backhand box. Then put a second target way over on the backhand corner and way over on the forehand corner, so that you have three inner tubes on the court.

With fifty or a hundred balls in your basket, try to hit your serves inside the inner tubes. Try a hard flat serve, then a spin second serve, mixing them up, down the line to the target in the center of the court, then to the two outside targets.

You must spend a lot of time practicing, as well as playing, if you want to improve your serve.

Unfortunately most people don't want to practice, they just want to get out there and play. I strongly recommend that you go to a pro. Tell him, "I've read Bobby Riggs's book and I want to learn defensive tennis, airtight tennis." If you do that, he can help to improve your game with a minimum of practice. He'll know you want to learn how to win against opponents who are faster and stronger.

THE RETURN OF SERVE

The return of serve is a vitally important shot. You must get the ball in play the way *you* can, not the way Smith, Laver or Gonzales can. Return the ball the best way you know how.

Don't go for a difficult shot. Take your position around the center of the service box about a foot inside the baseline. It is very important that you keep your eye on the ball and follow its flight. This will sharpen your anticipation. The minute the ball leaves your opponent's racket, you can begin to move toward the spot it is going to land.

Then hit the ball *safely*, with no risk involved, deep and high. Then you push right back to the center of the court. The thing to do is to push off early, either way, to get a very quick jump. Don't wait until the last moment to start moving to the ball. Try to move the instant it leaves your opponent's racket. In that way you will reach the ball in plenty of time to hit it within your framework of speed and control.

Hit the ball as hard as you can and still control it. If your opponent has come to the net and you need a little pace, hit the ball a little harder. But don't gamble on the shot. Let your opponent take all the risks.

THE DROP SHOT

The drop shot is a good shot for the weekend player to work on. It is not an easy shot to make. You should never attempt to make it unless you are a yard or two *inside* your own baseline and your opponent is at least a yard or two *behind* his baseline. This is the fundamental ground rule for trying the drop shot. This is the position play. Some people try a drop shot when they are behind their own baseline and the opponent is inside his. This is wrong.

A drop shot basically is a sacrifice. It should be used when you are way behind or way ahead and you are trying to wear out your opponent by making him run. You may lose the immediate point but you will reap the benefits many games later, perhaps in the following set. It's a good shot to use on a hot day when your opponent is showing signs of tiring.

A good player knows that basically the drop shot is a losing percentage play. Top players don't expect to make the point on it. There is a slim chance, if you make the perfect shot. But most top players are fast enough to reach a drop shot and put it away.

It calls for a lot of practice and you do have to have a certain amount of touch. If you don't do it right, you are going to set the shot up for your opponent.

It calls for good judgment. To learn the drop shot is much more difficult than it is to lob.

THE LOB

The lob is a great weapon. If you're playing in a group, in doubles especially, where you're all pretty even, the lob is terribly important. I love to use the lob all the time. I recommend it, especially for people between forty-five and fifty-five. You lob and lob and lob. That upsets the opponents. They try to hit harder than they know how. You can drive them back, away from the net. Then you can come in and take the offensive position. So don't overlook the lob as a beautiful weapon, both offensively and defensively. You can even lob your return of service in doubles. It is often a surprise. It is also one of the easiest shots.

For some reason or other there is a stigma attached to lobbing: "Look at that guy lobbing—he's just a dinker, just a pusher." The social player doesn't want to be put in that category.

But remember that the object of the game is not to look good; the idea is to play a winning tactic. Don't be fooled. Don't get psyched into thinking you have to look good out there. The name of the game is winning. And if you can both win *and* look bad you can make some money, if, like me, you're not averse to a little action from time to time.

WARMING UP

During the warm-up, you have a good chance to throw your opponent off balance a bit. Don't feed him all those shots that will make him feel good. This is a bit of gamesmanship. You practice your shots over in the corner and you hardly hit the ball to the guy at all. Some people get a little annoyed at this. But a lot of people won't understand what's going on. The first thing you know, you start the match and the guy hasn't hit a shot yet. He's not warmed up at all. And he doesn't know why it takes him so long to get going.

Now, if you recall, I did this with Margaret Court. She loves to warm up well. She likes to get into a groove. She has a beautiful stroke. But I was practicing my serve, first on one side, then the other. Banging the ball over here and over there. I hardly hit a ball to her.

And don't forget, I was well warmed up. I had had three practice sessions with Lornie Kuhle in the morning. I had hit a lot of serves, overheads, volleys.

She took a very light warm-up, on the other hand. Then we came out for the big TV audience and had to start promptly on time. Very few people picked that up at all. It was a deliberate tactic on my part.

PLAYING CONDITIONS

Wind

Bad conditions, such as a strong wind, help the lesser player. Wind is an equalizer. Tie breakers also help the lesser player because they shorten a match. Any time you put anything on sudden death, it's an equalizer. It's the same in golf, when they play sudden death after seventy-two holes to break a tie. Nicklaus is not the favorite to win in two or three holes that he would be in an eighteen-hole playoff.

If you have a baseball game that goes 9 all and into extra innings, the lesser team has more of a chance. Any time you shorten a game, the lesser team gets an edge. Even in football, it is going to help the underdog team—one pass, a break of some kind and a winning touchdown. Perfect conditions help the better player.

When you're downwind, you have an advantage, of course. The wind is at your back and the ball is going to get over to your opponent's side faster, with more pace, because you're going to use the wind. And the opponent has to hit against the wind, so he has no pace at all. You can run your opponent ragged if you have him downwind.

When you are playing against the wind you have a chance to hit much harder than you normally do. If your opponent goes to the net, you can throw up a high deep lob. You might be afraid the ball is going out, but you'll be surprised how often the wind will hold it up and drop it right at the baseline.

Serving with the wind, I use a lot of spin on the ball; against the wind I hit the ball very flat and hard.

A drop shot is very effective against the wind, because it will blow right back into the net. But with the wind, a short shot is not so effective since it will be blown back to your opponent.

Sun

When the sun is in the eyes of your opponent, be sure to use the lob, the old faithful "sun ball." Even the best of players have a hard time shading their eyes with their left hand. And a visor or hatbrim won't protect them from a high lob into the sun. It discourages an opponent from going to the net; it shakes him up. Let a bright sun work to your advantage, especially against a person who has to win from the net position.

A good tip in choosing sides on a very sunny day is this: If your opponent wins the toss and first serve, select the worse side, with the sun in your eyes. Then when you change courts after the first game, you will have two successive games with the sun behind you and you may reap a quick advantage from this.

Heat

You have to use your head in extremely hot, muggy conditions. You have to know something about your opponent. Does this person have more endurance than you have? If so, your tactic might be to try for quicker points. Be more aggressive than normal and try to get the points over with, so that you don't get caught in long exchanges in a drawn-out match.

But if your opponent lacks stamina and tires easily, play to keep him out in the sun. Prolong the rallies on purpose, slow the game down. After a while he's just going to wilt. I've known a lot of players like that who just can't take the humidity and the sun. I happen to like it. Under these conditions I love to slow down the pace of the match.

But if you're in a situation where the sun or humidity is tiring you, there are lots of ways to slow down the game. You can bounce the ball several times, very deliberately, before serving. When reaching to pick up a ball, you can kick it as if by accident and take your time about retrieving it. Bend down and tighten a shoelace and take a long time doing it. At the changeover sit down—play is supposed to be continuous, but this rule is enforced only at Wimbledon or Forest Hills—towel off and take your time about walking out to the baseline to resume play. Someone with experience can slow the game down in a hundred different ways.

This can be a bit of gamesmanship. If your opponent senses you are doing this, he may become annoyed and this will not be good for his tennis. Stalling can break an opponent's concentration. Frank Kovacs was notorious for this type of thing. He was a master at needling his opponent, staging sit-down strikes and so forth over line calls.

But although I have a reputation for gamesmanship, I never in my career set out deliberately to get someone's goat, to annoy him. Whatever I did was always designed to help *me*. I was tired, needed to catch my breath, so I would slow the game down and take some liberties. But I never did it with the idea of annoying my opponent, whatever people suspected.

DIFFERENT SURFACES

Alter your game to suit the surface you are playing on. On slow *clay* hit the ball easier than you normally would. Play more from the back of the court and try to be as steady as possible. Hit the high lob and use more drop shots. Play more defensively on clay. Do not serve at top speed.

On fast *cement* and other *hard courts* you get a big payoff with a big serve. It comes in fast, so you should hit it hard. Get to the net as often as you can and play more aggressively. Follow your short balls, as well as your serve, to the net.

On *grass* this becomes even more pronounced. The winning tactic is to hit as many balls as you can in the air. Don't let the ball bounce if you can help it; you may get a bad bounce. But you also want to rush your opponent and give him less chance to make a shot. You want to get to the net because any good volley on grass can be put away for a winner.

Grass has always been my best surface. This is contrary to what all the experts have believed. They said I was a clay-court specialist. I was known as a retriever, a defensive player. That's true. That would ordinarily mean I was best on clay.

But no matter how good you are defensively, you still have to have the offensive capacity to go with it. You cannot win on just pure defense alone.

Grass picked up my offense. It gave me equality with Budge and Kramer in the volleying area. I would come in and volley on grass and the ball would die. I only needed to hit a medium volley. I didn't come in and punch the ball the way a Rosewall, Hoad and Kramer did. With my light touch on the volley on cement and on clay, the ball would come up. A good fast player could get over there and get another crack at it. Then I would volley the ball and he'd get another crack at it. But on grass I would hit the volley and it was all over. No matter how fast the opponent, it was all over. The ball didn't come up. So grass is a one-volley shot. I had a beautiful technique on the volley. It wasn't severe. But on grass it was severe enough.

Another thing, grass is so dead you get nothing but low bounces, and I'm a terrific low-ball hitter.

I have a very deceptive serve, and grass picks up my serve. It takes the spin. My drop shot is deadly on the grass. Grass helped my lob too. It gave me equality with the offensive player. But despite my personal success on grass, I think it is a false game. I think grass courts should be torn up. This is happening at Forest Hills, and they should tear them up at Wimbledon and the rest of the world. A universal surface should be adopted for all tournament play, Davis Cup competition and other international contests. I would prefer a hard court, cement or asphalt or plastic, that produces a slow, low bounce. The court should also be kind on your feet.

KINDS OF RACKETS

It's difficult to find the racket that gives you the right feel. Tennis players are like baseball players when they get a bat they like. I am reminded of Rod Laver's experience with rackets a couple of years ago. He had a contract to use a certain metal racket in the United States. He was playing in the Madison Square Garden Classic for more than $100,000 in a series of matches, and he preferred to use his old English wood racket. So he had the wood racket painted gold to look like the metal one and went on to win all the money. The metal racket manufacturer was unhappy when the press discovered the switch and printed the story.

I know lots of players who get psyched out on rackets. I am among them. I've only had two or three rackets in my life that I really liked. I've been using steel or aluminum rackets for the past four or five years, experimenting, and have never gone back to the wood. Using wood now is like trying to swim upstream. I find it takes more strength and more effort to play with the wood. At my age I'm not that strong. I don't want to play with anything that forces me to work harder. With wood, the ball doesn't go as deep in the court for me. It's not as lively. But with metal you just have to brush the ball. It has a more resilient feel. The ball is livelier; with less effort, it goes faster.

My metal racket is lighter than the wooden ones I used when I was in my prime as an amateur and on the pro tour. A lighter racket is better for the older player. Pancho Gonzales in recent years has used an aluminum racket that weighs thirteen ounces, no more than a girl's racket. This way Pancho gets all the power he needs with less effort.

DOUBLES

Doubles is the best game for us middle-aged oldsters. It is not nearly as strenuous as singles. You have a partner alongside you, so you only have to cover half the court. There is a lot of net play, more volleying and lobbing than in singles. Doubles can be played offensively—as in the ranks of the tournament players—or defensively. It's amazing how effective defensive tactics can be.

I learned this the hard way in a tournament for fifty-and-over players in Knoxville several years ago. I was almost 6-0, 6-0, better than either of our opponents and my partner, Chauncey Steele, Jr., was 6-2, 6-2, better than either of them. So you'd think our combination was a dead cinch to win. We certainly thought so. But our opponents lobbed almost every ball, including return of service. The sun was high in the sky and we nearly went blind looking up in the sun court. Our opponents refused to give us a shot we could hit out for a winner. The upshot, after more than two and a half hours of neck-stretching sky balls, was a three-set victory for the lobbers.

In doubles you must get your first serve in play and follow it to the net. Keep the ball down the middle. Don't try an angle shot unless it's a sure putaway. The rule is down the middle with all shots until you have a chance to put the ball away.

Don't go for aces in serving. In airtight tennis you want to get 80 percent of your first serves in play. And don't give your opponents the opportunity to hit your second serve for winners.

In returning serve, keep the ball in play and low at your opponent's feet. Don't return so slowly that the player at the net can run over, poach and knock your return away.

As I pointed out, good lobbing is very important in doubles, even on the return of serve. A lob return right over the net man's head is a very good shot, especially in club and weekend tennis. It drives the opponents back and lets you take over the net position, which is the strong position in doubles. Don't be too proud to use the lob. It's a very effective shot.

Although you should go to the net behind service in doubles if you can, especially on cement and other hard surfaces, this is not so important on the slower clay courts. You can serve and stay at the baseline, in the older ranks, and still have a lot of fun. One partner can park at the net and the other stay back until he is drawn forward by a short ball. You are not going to win any tournaments or championships by staying back on your serve, but you are probably playing with other people who play the same way.

However, the orthodox method, the ABC of doubles, is to serve and go in for the volley, rather than take the return on the bounce. But that is for the younger players. Nowadays, in senior doubles, I do not automatically come in behind service, nor do my fellow seniors. Sometimes we do and sometimes we don't. We mix it up, especially on slower courts.

People often ask me how to decide which doubles partner plays the deuce court and which one the advantage court. It is not necessarily true that the player with the good backhand automatically goes into the ad court. The *stronger* player should play the left or ad court, for several reasons. He can take balls down the middle—key shots in doubles—on his forehand. And if an advantage point comes up for saving a game or winning a game, the stronger player is there to handle it.

Generally speaking, however, the good left-handed player takes the ad court with a right-handed partner. The southpaw can take the opponents' American twist service on his forehand and make a good cross-court return, a tough shot for a right-hander.

In doubles it's a good idea to talk up the game with your partner. Never moan or groan when he makes a mistake. He undoubtedly feels worse than you do about his errors. Encourage him by complimenting him on his good shots. And don't be shy about yelling "Mine!" if you have a better shot at the ball. The same thing goes for "Yours!" if the ball is over your head or out of reach. And if the ball seems to be sailing wide or long, as your partner is poised to hit it, yell "Out!" This may annoy your opponents, but it's within the rules and can mean the difference between winning or losing a point.

George Lott, one of the greatest doubles players of all time, once said, "Doubles is mainly a matter of getting a service break, then hanging on for dear life." To get that all-important service break, concentrate on returning every serve, take the net away from your opponents, force them to hit up to you and you'll do it somehow.